Skyrocketing
SALES!

Skyrocketing
SALES!

The Ultimate Guide to Boosting Your Confidence and Exceeding Your Goals

DEBBIE ALLEN

Dearborn™
Trade Publishing
A **Kaplan Professional** Company

President, Dearborn Publishing: Roy Lipner
Vice President and Publisher: Cynthia A. Zigmund
Senior Acquisitions Editor: Michael Cunningham
Development Editor: Karen Murphy
Senior Project Editor: Trey Thoelcke
Interior Design: Lucy Jenkins
Cover Design: Sue Giroux
Typesetting: Ellen Gurak

Published by Dearborn Trade Publishing
A Kaplan Professional Company

Library of Congress Cataloging-in-Publication Data

Allen, Debbie, 1953-
    Skyrocketing sales! : the ultimate guide to boosting your confidence
and exceeding your goals / Debbie Allen.
       p. cm.
    Includes index.
    ISBN-13: 978-1-4195-1048-9
    1. Selling.   I. Title.
    HF5438.25.A42 2005
    658.85–dc22
                          2005018374

PRAISE FOR *SKYROCKETING SALES!*

*Debbie Allen has done it again as she's done it in the past—
provided solid business principles that win friends and generate
profits.*
**JAY CONRAD LEVINSON,
AUTHOR OF THE GUERRILLA MARKETING SERIES OF BOOKS**

DON'T WASTE YOUR TIME reading Skyrocketing Sales! . . .
*UNLESS you are actually committed to taking your sales to the
next level. If your sales results need super-charging, then this book
will help you. You can read just one chapter and you'll get more
than your money's worth. So don't waste your time! Get this book
IMMEDIATELY and read it! Then watch your sales soar!*
JOEL WELDON, INTERNATIONAL SPEAKER AND BUSINESS EXPERT

*Where was this book when I first started my sales career? It would
have cut years off my learning curve. Anyone who reads*
Skyrocketing Sales! *will quickly join the ranks of the top
performers.*
**JOE BONURA, AUTHOR OF *THROW THE RABBIT: THE ULTIMATE APPROACH
TO THREE-DIMENSIONAL SELLING***

*Debbie Allen takes the personal side of selling out of the clouds and
into the real world. She guides readers beyond skills and techniques
to helping them make allies with what can make or break their
success—their brains.*
**MARCIA REYNOLDS, AUTHOR OF *OUTSMART YOUR BRAIN! HOW TO MAKE
SUCCESS FEEL EASY***

*Debbie has done it again! She has put together the ultimate tool for
anyone who has to sell anything to anybody. The secrets and
strategies contained in this book will move people forward in the
direction of their dreams.*
MARK LEBLANC, AUTHOR OF *GROWING YOUR BUSINESS!*

Now Finally, Debbie Allen reveals her time-tested secret recipe for superior selling–a rare blend of personality, know-how, expertise, and motivation. Implement the pearls of wisdom featured in this guide and you'll win sales contests for years to come.

ERIC GELB, INTERNATIONALLY-RECOGNIZED COPYWRITER AND AUTHOR OF *THE PROFIT PUMP*

Debbie Allen has, by this time, established herself as one of today's most dynamic and clever experts on sales and self-promotion. I learn something new and re-learn what I haven't thought of for a while–every time I pick up one of her books.

BOB BURG, AUTHOR OF *ENDLESS REFERRALS* AND *WINNING WITHOUT INTIMIDATION*

This book is an excellent resource for anyone selling anything! It will build your sales confidence, motivate you to exceed your goals, and trigger your mind to think about sales differently from this day forward! Grab a copy now–for everyone on your sales team!

JOSEPH SUGARMAN, AUTHOR OF *TRIGGERS: 30 SALES TOOLS YOU CAN USE TO CONTROL THE MIND OF YOUR PROSPECT TO MOTIVATE, INFLUENCE, AND PERSUADE*

C o n t e n t s

WHY SHOULD YOU READ THIS BOOK?

This powerful book will inspire you to reach your peak sales potential. You will discover how easy and enjoyable selling can be when you replace ineffective traditional sales strategies with effective relationship-building strategies.

Imagine never having to worry about achieving your sales goals ever again. Imagine enjoying selling and servicing your customers so much that you can't wait to get to work every day. Imagine avoiding past sales frustrations and easily managing customer resistance with conversational selling strategies instead of high-pressure, conventional sales strategies that have failed you in the past.

Imagine that this book will change the way you think about selling forever. But don't just read this book—study it, because your sales and profits depend on it! Try out the principles and beliefs for yourself. See what works for you and keep doing it.

My goal of writing this book is to empower you to a more positive way of thinking and acting to stimulate more sales opportunities than you can handle. That would be a good problem to have—wouldn't it?

If your subconscious mind-set is not in tune with positive, supportive beliefs about selling, nothing you learn about sales, nothing you already know about sales, and nothing you do to reach your goals will make much of a difference.

Some people are destined to struggle with sales their entire life, and barely make enough to pay their bills each month; while others are making millions selling high-end items and loving every minute of it. Why is this? Is it because they are born salespeople who naturally have what it takes? Hardly!

It is because these individuals have a strong belief not only in themselves, but in the products or services they sell as well. They hold a positive belief about what their products and services can do to help others get what they want, solve their problems, and/or improve their lives in some way. They love selling, and feel amazingly comfortable building valuable relationships based around their sales expertise. These sales experts have a positive belief system based around selling, and know how to effectively promote themselves and their products in the service of others.

This book offers you strategies that will give you the same unlimited potential once you expand your mind to a new way of thinking. By developing a new belief system about selling, you will begin to move to a higher level of success—a level that will allow you to overcome personal obstacles and barriers existing in your current belief system that rob you of the sales you deserve. Once you reach this level you will begin to stop sabotaging opportunities and start to reap the rewards that will skyrocket your sales and you will continually exceed your goals.

The innovative tips and strategies shared in this book will allow you to develop an unstoppable belief system within yourself. When your belief system becomes more positive—your sales confidence will soar!

As you learn to enjoy the sales process more with your newly discovered belief system, your customer relationships will begin to magnify. You will begin to reap a steady stream of endless referrals, raving testimonials, and powerful word-of-mouth advertising.

As your confidence continues to build, you will move past any fears of selling that were previously programmed into your belief system. We all have some form of sales call reluctance that holds us back from initiating more sales opportunities.

You will discover what may be holding you back from reaching your sales expectations and exceeding your goals. Once discovered, you will learn how to practice new habits that will allow you to move past the fears, obstacles, and challenges you may have.

The step-by-step approach offered in this book will make it easy for you to initiate more effective selling habits. You will learn to rid yourself of negative, ineffective beliefs about selling, and instantly begin to relate to a more workable way of selling for life.

As you develop these new sales skills, your enthusiasm and service-oriented behaviors will quickly persuade more people to buy from you, to refer you, and to continue to do business with you.

Words on a page cannot necessarily transform a person, but if you are open to a new way of thinking, this book can and will dramatically change your life.

Begin your journey now by opening your mind to a new way of thinking and to endless sales opportunities!

Just about the time I had come to the conclusion that I needed to write a book on sales, I got an e-mail from an agent in New York who discovered me on a Google search, wanting to know if I would be interested in writing a book on sales.

If you have any idea how hard it is to find an agent, much less one that will even talk to you, you know that getting discovered on Google is a rare thing—especially when they are ready to find you a book deal after a short, 20-minute phone conversation.

I've read dozens and dozens of sales books over the years focusing on outdated, traditional sales methods and high-pressure sales strategies, and most of them never taught me much in my 30+ years of selling. I would try a tip here and there from these books, but never felt truly comfortable with the "closing" and "pitch" strategies they shared. Far more interesting to me was a book on "sales motivation."

Thank you to Michael Cunningham at Dearborn Trade Publishing, for your support of my ideas, and for leading me through the process like the pro that you are.

Finally, I am deeply grateful to all of my sales mentors and business alliances over the years for sharing their wealth of wisdom, support, and testament to *Skyrocketing Sales!*

Debbie Allen has been in sales for more than 30 years. One of her first jobs was selling used rental cars when she was just 19 years old. From that day forward, she was motivated to sell—products, services, and even her own companies.

For more than 10 years, Debbie has shared her sales and marketing expertise as an international business speaker. She addresses over 75 organizations and more than 50,000 people each year in numerous countries around the world, sharing her expertise. As a serial entrepreneur, Debbie has built and sold six highly successful businesses. Her acute business sense, high energy, and great sense of humor are teamed up with her enthusiasm to make her a dynamic presenter.

As an internationally acclaimed motivational speaker, Debbie knows how to touch the minds and hearts of her audiences. She provides practical, easy-to-follow sales strategies that can help anyone become more successful in both their personal life and in their professional life.

She has been a member of the National Speakers Association since 1995, and has achieved the honor of Certified Speaking Professional (CSP) for her professional platform skills, an honor achieved by less than 10 percent of all members.

Debbie is a recipient of *The Blue Chip Enterprise Award*, sponsored by the National Chamber of Commerce and presented for overcoming business obstacles and achieving fast business growth. Her sales expertise has been featured in *Entrepreneur, Selling Power, Sales & Marketing Excellence*, and the *National Encyclopedia of Experts*.

Debbie is an award-winning author of five books including *Skyrocketing Sales!*, *Confessions of Shameless Self Promoters*, *Confessions of Shameless Internet Promoters*, and others.

Believing in YOU and selling yourself effectively is the KEY to sales success!

COMPLETE SALES CONFIDENCE

1

THE AMAZING POWER OF YOUR BELIEF SYSTEM

"To believe with certainty we must begin with doubting."
STANISLAUS LESCYNSKI

Uncovering your personal thoughts and beliefs will help you to understand how you may be limiting your own sales success. Your beliefs are equivalent to how you think and act every day with everything you do. Your beliefs have amazing powers that set the level of success you will create automatically.

This book will allow you to uncover the beliefs that hold you back from initiating more sales opportunities. You are just like everyone else—we all have beliefs that limit us in some way or another. The first step in overcoming the obstacles that hold us back is AWARENESS. Use this book as your awareness guide, to discover how and why your current beliefs and thoughts may be holding you back from achieving more.

"I have no riches but my thoughts,
yet these are wealth enough to me."
SARA TEASDALE

This awareness will guide you and help you reprogram any negative beliefs and/or fears that are currently sabotaging you from exceeding your sales goals. It will allow you to build the confidence you need to present your own style, uniqueness, essence, and magnificence and to stand out amongst your competitors.

How you think and what you believe to be true about yourself will automatically be directed by how well or how poorly you sell. We all think differently, and we all have different belief systems that cause us to react and respond differently. Therefore, no two belief systems and no two salespeople are alike.

That is why I wanted to write a sales book that would get into your mind and into your personal beliefs first and foremost.

What you think and believe to be true is.

By getting to the root of your personal beliefs first, I can offer you systems and strategies that will dramatically improve your sales. Your beliefs are incredibly flexible, generous, and capable. Whatever you sincerely ask of your beliefs, you will become.

You've probably read too many books that focus on high-pressure, traditional selling strategies that are completely ineffective. I've read dozens of them, and have gotten very few tips and strategies that fit the type of selling that is effective for me. So why do these high-pressure, "pitch" sales books still sell? Because we have thousands of car salespeople who still know how to read! Okay, so not all car salespeople play the high-pressure game, but they tend to be the first type of salesperson we think of when we think of high-pressure selling—right?

THE "BELIEVE I KNOW IT ALL" SABOTAGE

You may be new to sales or have been selling for years. What I'm going to ask of you, my friend, is to simply let go of believing you are RIGHT about how to sell as you read this book. Be willing to let go of having to do it your way. Why? Because your way is not enough or you would not be reading this book. If you already have achieved every sales goal and won every award, you are doing a lot of things right, but you obviously want more.

You've probably heard the saying, "When you think you know it all—you're right; that is all you will ever know." I don't think that I really related to that statement until later in life, because, as the saying goes, "With age comes wisdom." At least when our age begins to fade from us, it is replaced with wisdom, confidence, and, sometimes, even patience. A fair trade!

> *"The older we grow, the greater becomes our wonder."*
> **MARK TWAIN**

My lack of patience and young, know-it-all attitude held me back from making the most out of selling much of my adult life. Sure, I was good at selling; and believe me, I sold a lot, but I certainly had a lot of room for growth and improvement. That cost me a lot in lost sales opportunities over the years.

Because I used to do the same thing, it is now easy for me to spot people in my audiences who are still getting in their own way and sabotaging sales opportunities. They come into the presentation with their arms crossed, leaning back in their chairs, with sober faces staring back at me, and thinking, "What does this blonde have to tell me about sales that I don't already know? This is a waste of my time. I've been selling for years and making great money at it."

These sales know-it-alls have a belief system that talks to them like this, in self-sabotaging language: "You don't need to listen to another sales presentation or read another sales book because, frankly, it is beneath you."

One group of salespeople stands out in my mind when I think of know-it-alls. I was presenting a seminar for a small group of about 75 (mostly male) high-level salespeople knocking out six-figure-plus incomes. It was going well, and the vast majority of the group was hanging on my every word; however, one person in particular was not only the know-it-all, he was the heckler as well.

As I addressed different points, he would shout out comments and objections. He believed in high-pressure selling, and that was the only way he believed in selling. It was obviously working for him to some degree, because he was pulling in big numbers. But was he missing opportunities to sell to people who didn't buy from his style of selling? You bet he was!

After two hours of his heckling, objecting, and shouting out, he asked if he could have one of my books for free when I was passing some out as gifts to audience members who participated in exercises and helped out during my presentation. With a light-hearted smile on my face, I said in front of the group, "No, sorry, but I don't give out bonuses for hecklers." This comment surprised him and took him a bit off guard as I called him on his behavior in front of the group in a nice way.

That evening my client treated the entire sales team and myself to dinner at a fun, relaxed restaurant. Shortly after everyone was seated for dinner, the "heckler" came over to my table and asked if he could talk with me for a few minutes. I said, "Sure, what's on your mind?"

He replied, "I just wanted to tell you how much I enjoyed your presentation today. It really made me think about how to sell. Because my sales always top the charts over the majority of the sales team, I thought that my way of selling was the best and only way to sell. But today you opened my mind to another way of thinking. I do know that my high-pressure methods have turned off some clients, but I always want to win the sale, and maybe that is why I often feel I need to add the pressure. I really am a good guy, enjoy my customers, make friends with most of them, and love to sell. Maybe that is why I have gotten away with some of my high-pressure, go-for-the-jugular approaches in the past." He gave me a big hug and thanked me.

We must all stay open-minded to new ideas and new ways of selling, because as soon as you think you have it all figured out, your customer changes. The economy changes, products change, services change, and competitors change too. That is also what makes sales so challenging, interesting, and rewarding at the same time. There is nothing quite like the feeling of the HIGH from a big sale when both you and your customer are equally thrilled with the purchase.

In my early years of selling, I was focused only on what I wanted: my goals and making a buck first, and the customer second. This added a lot of pressure and stress on me and, therefore, I didn't really like selling. But there was no way around it; every business and everything I did revolved around selling my products, my services, and myself.

Personally, I didn't really get good at selling until I finally got out of my own way and began to open up myself to new thoughts and beliefs, both internally and externally. As I opened up to new beliefs, I also began to open up to my customers, and my sales took off like a rocket.

Learning to expand our minds to new thoughts, beliefs, and creativity is an amazingly empowering thing.

Do I have your commitment to being open-minded as you read this book?

Good, because your mind is where everything begins. It will guide you and lead you in the direction of success or of failure. It will motivate you or depress you. It offers the tools and support that can help you increase sales over sales skills alone—but only if you allow it to guide you.

ARE YOU MAKING EXCUSES OR ARE YOU MAKING SALES?

Your personal belief system will either move you ahead—or hold you back. Period!

The power of your belief system truly is amazing! It is like your own personal barometer that gauges the power (or lack of it) in your subconscious mind every day. Yet beliefs and thoughts are only in your subconscious mind.

Most of our beliefs have been programmed deeply into our minds since childhood. Therefore, we all act and feel according to what we believe to be true about ourselves and our environment, based on beliefs formed when growing up.

Many of these beliefs and thoughts, however, are negative and self-defeating. We all have negative self-talk from time to time, nagging at us and beating up our confidence even after we work so hard to build it up.

The good news is that you are an adult now, and you have the ability to take control of these voices in your head.

You can either choose to blame your environment and make excuses for it and your lack of sales—or, you can accept the fact that you are in control and have the ability to think and act positively in any sales environment.

You have the ability to change your beliefs, your thoughts, and your actions. Only you can allow yourself to move past old, negative ways of thinking. You have the ability to move away from any self-destructive, self-sabotaging talk that creates barriers along the path of your success.

Once you realize that your thoughts, feelings, and actions are all the result of your self-image and personal beliefs, you can then, and only then, begin to move past the behaviors that are holding you back from reaching your peak sales potential.

When you develop a positive mind-set about selling, you instantly begin to break down negative and limited belief systems. Barriers and obstacles that once may have limited your sales success begin to move away.

Here are some real-life negative comments that I hear from salespeople, business owners, and managers all the time. Listen up! If you are hearing any of these in your head, you had better lock down your brain and rid yourself of these thieves that are robbing you from sales success and get rid of them fast!

- I'm just no good at selling.
- How am I ever going to measure up to _____?
- The economy is not good in the area and sales are down.
- Ever since _____, I can't seem to get my sales back on track.
- The weather is keeping everyone away.
- Business is slow—there is just no traffic in this mall.
- The landlords don't do anything to promote the center.
- I don't handle rejection well, therefore, I avoid it at all costs.
- Because I don't want to appear pushy or intrusive, I avoid promoting myself.
- I don't want to promote myself as an expert because I don't know enough yet.
- How come I get all the "pain in the rear" customers?
- There is too much competition in my industry right now.

Excuses, excuses, excuses! Now I'm sure that the vast majority of the time you don't have negative and/or ineffective comments like these flying out of your mouth, but occasionally, we all do. It is just human nature. The sad thing is that most of us don't even recognize this as negative self-talk, nor do we understand what this type of talk does to our belief programming.

Negative self-talk kills opportunities for success!

The worse part about negative self-talk is when we can't stop it from flowing out of our mouths at times. In fact, we may repeat it so often, we believe it to be true. We program our beliefs to accept this negative talk as the truth. It is these ineffective words, however, that kill your opportunities to close more sales.

Speaking negative, unhealthy words out loud only damages your belief system even more. Once self-defeating thoughts leak out of our heads and into the form of affirmations, we sabotage both our personal success and our professional success.

Negative affirmations also are extremely damaging to your self-confidence. Positive affirmations, on the other hand, are amazingly empowering.

We become what we think about most!

Affirmations are one of the most important elements of creative visualization. To "affirm" means to make firm. An affirmation is a strong statement that something is already so. It is a way of making firm that which you are imagining. If you imagine failure, you will allow negative forces to come to you that will continue to make you fail and lose more sales.

Positive and empowering affirmations allow the universe to reward you with unlimited opportunities and abundance. We all have opportunities to become more successful, yet the negative mind discards them long before they have a chance to blossom and grow.

The idea behind affirmations is that through the repetition of positive statements, we can improve our self-respect, make greater progress toward growth, and, in general, increase our magnetism to success. To progress in sales, a positive self-image is essential.

As soon as you judge yourself, you are back to limited sales success and limited beliefs.

To expand your self-image, replace limited beliefs with powerful affirmations, feelings, and actions.

To affirm is to state that it is so. As you maintain this attitude of your belief system as true, regardless of all evidence to the contrary, you will receive a response. Repeating an affirmation, knowing what you are saying and why you are saying it, will lead your belief system to a state of consciousness where it becomes reality. Keep on affirming that you are a dynamic salesperson who can and will exceed any goals you set before you. As you repeat your affirmation over and over again, allow your subconscious mind to catch up and go to work on your behalf.

Triumphs are won in your mind first!

Now take your affirmation to another level. Speak your affirmations out loud. Share them with people who support your success. If you are like most of us, you will probably let yourself down before letting others down. By sharing your sales goals out loud with others, you allow yourself to step up to a higher level of commitment toward these goals. What you focus on most becomes reality!

Don't bother sharing your affirmations, beliefs, and goals with negative people. These dream stealers are negative forces that rob you of personal growth and empowerment. Often, they come in the form of doomsayers who enjoy wallowing in their own self-pity. They focus on what-ifs and limited beliefs.

Because they enjoy the company of like-minded people, they will work hard at keeping you down at their level. Don't be tempted to go down there. Refuse to allow them to influence your beliefs.

You become who you surround yourself with.

One of my biggest pet peeves is negative-thinking people. I simply cannot afford to be around them. I refuse to allow them to rob me of my positive beliefs, lofty goals, and aspirations— and neither should you! Any negative thought is multiplied. Negative issues outweigh positives. For example, take a look at the news we hear every day. Most of it is negative. We are bombarded with negative forces around us so much that we have to work very hard to keep our positive mind-sets in check.

We all know negative people. They are the ones who focus more on what will or could go wrong than on what will go right. These are the salespeople who look for every opportunity to focus on why sales are down, how bad business is, how hard it is to make ends meet, why you get all the breaks instead of them, and so on. These damaging forces dramatically affect their belief systems. Some of them have negative vibes so deeply ingrained into their own beliefs that everything they touch turns sour.

Watch out for negative people. They will want to keep you down instead of lifting you up. They will tell you that you are crazy and will try to bring you down to their level of thinking to hold you back from moving beyond them. They will tell you that you are crazy when you come up with innovative ideas or dare to break the mold or try something different.

I've been told I was crazy way too many times. At first I questioned it, but almost every time I was told that, the opposite was actually true. Instead, I was refusing to conform, challenging old beliefs, and empowering my mind to a new way of thinking. This crazy strategy has paid off for me many times over in my numerous sales opportunities.

Do you know why people tell you that you are crazy? Because your innovative ideas, positive thinking, and out-of-the-box concepts scare them. They could not perceive your ideas with their own negative beliefs. Why? Because they don't have the same vision, guts, or positive outlook that you do! Therefore, being crazy often can be a good thing.

Watch out for jealous people too. They appear to be your friends, all the time trying to get you to conform and convert back to their level of thinking so that they can feel more comfortable with their own limited success. You'll see this to be true when your sales skyrocket beyond those negative people very quickly.

But watch out, because those slippery devils will try to reel you back in to the negative trap at any moment. I've seen it happen for years with my own sales staff.

Dream stealers, doomsayers, what-ifers, and jealous people who don't support you must be avoided at all costs if you are serious about skyrocketing your sales!

DAD'S LESSON IN POSITIVE THINKING

When I was growing up, my dad had a long career as a successful car salesperson. He created a very nice living for my family that allowed us to take long vacations, eat out at fine restaurants, and live in a nice house. Dad made selling look like an easy job. All I knew was that he showed up and made good money.

Dad never told me how hard it was for him to get going in sales and to fit in with the other car salespeople until I told him I was writing this book. Then he shared his story with me.

Back in the mid-1950s when he started in sales, he didn't have a positive belief system in himself or in his abilities. What he did have was a commitment to learning quickly and doing whatever it took to make it in sales. Searching for a way to build up his confidence, he turned to books and motivational tapes.

Dad discovered a book that would be the turning point in his life: *The Power of Positive Thinking*, by Norman Vincent Peale. He listened to the words in the book as they spoke to him. These powerful words allowed him to rid himself of self-doubt, and freed him of worry, stress, and resentment. *The Power* helped him to rise above problems, visualizing solutions and eliminating all negative thoughts.

Dad truly believes this book changed him forever. Yet it wasn't actually the book itself that changed him, it was the habit-changing tools the book offered that allowed him to find a way to build a strong belief within himself. Dad was ready to rid himself of damaging self-doubt, and ready to move toward a more positive belief system. What changed him was that he was ready to change.

Shortly after reading *The Power*, Dad started working out and feeling good about himself. His newly modeled self-esteem gave him a whatever-it-takes attitude to become the top salesperson in his office month after month. When all the other salespeople were sitting around gossiping and making excuses for why there were no customers in the lot, Dad was making calls and getting innovative.

Dad created a big colorful board to keep track of his calls and systemize his business, and placed it on the wall in his office. Now do you think the other salespeople wanted to know how his new system was working so they could apply it too? No way! They just laughed at him and told him he was crazy!

Dad's positive attitude and self-confidence allowed him to ignore their negative comments and move ahead of them in sales. He also discovered that those negative salespeople also had a hard time being around him once his sales soared. So what did he do? He found a new set of positive friends and business associates to hang out with—people who pulled him up and supported his success.

Dad is one of the most positive people I know, and his contagious enthusiasm allows him to sell just about anything to anyone. Even when the worst possible scenario is placed in front of him, Dad finds a way to stay positive and rise above it. He's amazing!

Dad showed me that when you develop a positive belief system and begin to reach a high level of success in sales, nothing will hold you back. He also taught me to think outside-of-the-box and to take some risks.

Taking calculated risks is the only way to truly excel.

Most salespeople already have a heads-up on taking risks and being somewhat crazy by most people's standards. Often, they are nonconformists who don't want a job that dictates their salary or puts limits on them. Some of their parents may still be asking: "When are you going to get a real job?" Meaning, when are you going to conform to the dollar-per-hour, steady paycheck job. "NEVER!"

Selling allows you the freedom to create your own goals and to excel at whatever level you choose. Selling allows you the ability to create your own income and your own destiny.

Understand that along with this freedom come peaks and valleys, highs and lows, risks and rewards. You are your own self-motivator.

If it were easy, everyone would be doing it and doing it well. But that's not the case. You are an exception, and that is why developing a positive self-image and powerful belief system is so important to get you through the hard times as well as the good.

Developing a winning mind-set is the starting point in your journey to becoming a top sales performer.

SELF-PERCEPTION AWARENESS

Your self-perception is continually jaded by your belief system. Selling yourself on the ideas of what you believe to be true about how well you sell is critical to your success.

Take a few moments to evaluate your perception of how well you currently SELL. How do you perceive your success, your income, and your future right now? Keep in mind that a perception is simply an insight, viewpoint, opinion, or personal assessment of what you believe to be true. Stay positive and focused as you make note of your self-perception beliefs.

Three perceptions that relate to my level of success in sales right now are:

1. _____
2. _____
3. _____

Positive self-perception, or high self-esteem, is a desired outcome of your development process. It has even been linked to long-term mental health and to emotional well-being. It has been found that positive self-perception is generally associated with an approaching, flexible, and positive mood pattern, and with high task orientation.

"There are two good things in life: freedom of thought and freedom of action."
W. SOMERSET MAUGHAM

THE AUTO PILOT OF YOUR BELIEFS LIES IN YOUR SUBCONSCIOUS

Your self-image, or what you believe to be true about yourself in your subconscious mind, controls your destiny. Your subconscious mind is a powerful source that regulates everything in your life. It allows you to do things automatically, without conscious thought. It does not judge what is right or wrong. It only does what it has been programmed to do by your thoughts and beliefs.

Your subconscious mind speaks to you through intuition, impulses, hunches, intimations, urges, and ideas. It is always telling you to rise, transcend, grow, advance, adventure, and move forward to greater heights.

Your subconscious mind is never short of ideas. Within it there are an infinite number of ideas ready to flow into your conscious mind and appear as cash in your pocket in countless ways. Your subconscious never sleeps. It is always on the job.

Your subconscious does not say, "I don't want to do it." Instead, it reacts at lightning speed automatically as if you are in overdrive. For example, have you ever driven your car somewhere and completely forgotten how you got there? This was your subconscious at the wheel. Your subconscious mind allowed you to drive to that location by habit, while your conscious mind was still asleep or lost in a daydream somewhere.

Your conscious mind is rational, while your subconscious is irrational. Your subconscious mind is reactive—it responds automatically to your thoughts and beliefs. The subconscious is subject to the conscious mind. That is why it is called subconscious or subjective.

When your conscious mind is full of fear, worry, and anxiety, these negative emotions are released in your subconscious mind. They flood the subconscious mind with a sense of panic and despair. This is what you are feeling when you fear cold calling, attending sales meetings outside of your comfort zone, or not reaching your monthly goals.

So how do you take control of this fear and anxiety? By speaking affirmatively with a deep sense of authority to the irrational emotions generated in your deeper mind.

Speak up, because your subconscious will listen. Your brain takes the orders you give it based on what your conscious mind believes and accepts as true. It does not question the orders or the basis on which they are given, it simply reacts.

Never use negative expressions, such as "I'm not good enough" or "I can't do this," because when you speak these words you also are feeding damaging beliefs to your hungry subconscious mind.

For example, if you repeatedly say negative comments like "My sales are down and I can't seem to get out of the slump," your subconscious mind is going to start believing this statement as true, and it will follow your orders to sabotage your success.

It is important to realize that different people will react in different ways to the same suggestion. This is because they have different subconscious conditioning or beliefs. All of us have our own inner fears, beliefs, and opinions. These inner assumptions rule and govern our lives. You accept it mentally. Only at that point do subconscious powers begin to act according to your suggestions.

When you set up obstacles in your conscious mind, you are denying wisdom and intelligence to feed your subconscious. Once you start feeding negative thoughts, there is no way out of the roadblock you create in your mind. If you want your subconscious to work for you, you have to give it the RIGHT suggestions to get POSITIVE feedback that will move you beyond the barriers. Your subconscious is your friend and it works for you around the clock, 24/7. It is controlling your heartbeat and breathing at this very minute. It is keeping you alive. It is forever seeking to take care of you, preserve you, and grant your wishes.

Change your thoughts, and you change your destiny.

Remember that your subconscious mind does not engage in proving whether your thoughts are good or bad, true or false. It simply responds according to the nature of your mental suggestions. It does not have the ability to argue or dispute what it is told. Your subconscious mind will either support you or sabotage you. You choose.

So how do you begin to reprogram your subconscious? Wouldn't you love to have your own "sales genie," who could grant you a wish upon your command, along with you 24 hours a day? Well you do, so start believing in and asking for more positive outcomes—and your wishes will be granted.

Before you go to bed every night, feed your subconscious with positive affirmations: I wish to have another successful day in sales tomorrow and I know that I will. I have all the skills, knowledge, and support to make it happen. My sales confidence grows each day and I believe that I will exceed my goals.

Again, remember to be very careful and specific, because if you give the wrong information, you will sabotage your success instead of empowering yourself. Your subconscious only reacts to your beliefs and suggestions. Therefore, if you suggest negative beliefs, you grant yourself limitations and frustrations instead of unlimited success and joy.

2

BOOST YOUR
SALES CONFIDENCE

*"What you think of yourself is much more important than what
others think of you."*
SENECA

Before you can sell anything successfully, you must first sell your ideas, your wishes, your needs, your ambitions, your skills, your experience, your products, and your services—you must be absolutely SOLD on you.

Your confidence will never fail you. What can fail you, however, are those things in which you place your confidence.

In selling yourself successfully, absolute confidence in yourself is a must! Confidence, in turn, breeds courage. This being true, you must make sure that your self-confidence goes to work for you, because in selling ourselves, we are putting our confidence in ourselves.

Why is this so important to be successful in sales? Because if you don't have confidence in yourself, how can you expect prospective customers to have confidence and faith in you either?

You are what you believe. You are what you think.

YOU ARE THE GREATEST

Boxer Muhammad Ali made the line "I am the greatest!" famous. Before every fight he prepared himself by training both his body and his mind. He had such a strong belief in his abilities, and bravely dared to announce it to the world. By repeating his affirmation over and over again, he was training his subconscious to support his win.

His goal was to go for the world championship, and he trained hard every day to be his best. If you want to be a champion at selling, you must work every day too—even when you don't feel like it.

> *"I hated every minute of training, but I said, 'Don't quit. Suffer now and live the rest of my life as a champion.'"*
> **MUHAMMAD ALI**

"I dance like a butterfly and I sting like a bee ... I'll knock you down by round three." Ali took his affirmation one step further and visualized knocking down the other boxer in the ring by the third round. He was creating psychological warfare in the other boxer's mind at the same time.

The first time he fought Leon Spinks is the only time he did not go through this normal psyching-up affirmation process, and the world saw Muhammad Ali go down in defeat. By failing to sell himself on his beliefs that day, he lost the fight.

Repeat this affirmation out loud: "I am the greatest! I am the greatest!" Say it again and again every day until you believe it to be true.

Repeat these statements out loud: "My sales are improving every day. My greatest sales goals will be exceeded very soon." As you repeat these statements and believe them to be true, you feed both your conscious and subconscious mind with champion results.

SUCCESSFUL PEOPLE EXPECT TO SUCCEED

People who are successful have confidence in their abilities and creativity. Unsuccessful people, on the other hand, expect to fail. They lack confidence in themselves and their abilities. Because they lack the confidence in themselves, they see obstacles and are unwilling to take risks.

It's normal for salespeople to occasionally question, have doubt, and subsequently lose confidence regarding the superiority of their company, product, service, pricing, and even themselves. During these times of doubt, it's important to think back to all your successes, how you felt at that time, and why you felt that way. Let those positive feelings recharge and revitalize your beliefs that you and what you are selling are indeed the very best.

Everyone has confidence in something!

As we grow up we build up our confidence and self-esteem by accepting it from others. Some of us may have grown up with supportive family and friends that instilled in us a strong self-worth, while others may have had to learn it on their own.

Past conditioning and programming is also where most low self-esteem stems from. Even when parents mean well, they often program thoughts into their children that tear down their confidence instead of building it up.

Although good parents want to support their children's confidence, they still pass along negative words that tear it down. Negative words heard over and over again tend to bruise confidence and self-worth.

Remember how many "NOs" you heard when you grew up? You probably heard ten NOs to every one Yes. The word NO is probably one of the first words you and/or your own children spoke. Even after parents program the word NO into their children's heads day after day, they get frustrated when their children repeat it back to them. From the day we are born, we are bombarded with negative suggestions. Not knowing how to counter them, we unconsciously accept them and bring them into being as our experience.

Some negative statements do much more damage to confidence, such as "You're doing it wrong" versus "That's perfect, you're doing it great"; "You're stupid" versus "You're smart"; "You'll never amount to anything" versus "You're a winner." Negative statements such as these would make anyone feel that they don't stack up. And the sad thing about it is that more often than not these negative words turn into negative beliefs and stay with us well into our adult lives.

It is understandable why so few people reach their peak potential earnings or why they settle for relationships that are not positive influences; and, therefore, the pattern is repeated and limits are placed on self-worth. This also explains why so many people also sabotage their success over and over again.

Yet, you can't blame your parents. Blame won't get you anywhere in life. Most parents tend to be overly protective, so it's only natural for them to want their children to be more and to achieve more. Often they are unaware of how to communicate this into more positive words because of their own negative programming. Pay attention to your own self-talk. Does it repeat negative patterns learned from childhood? If so, stop and catch yourself. Change these words to more positive patterns that will support and build up your confidence.

Remember, you are an adult now; and you have the choice to adjust your programming, change your beliefs, and boost your confidence.

You and you alone have the responsibility to change old programming and beliefs.

Recognize that whether you are worthy or not is all a made-up belief. Nothing has meaning except for the meaning you give it. You and you alone determine if you're going to be worthy. It's simply your perspective. If you say you're worthy, you are. If you say you're not worthy, you're not. Stop buying into whether you are worthy or not and start taking actions you need to become more successful.

GROWING UP SELLING IN THE FAMILY BUSINESS

I grew up with amazingly supportive parents, yet somehow, measuring up to my brother was always a problem for me. I had to grow up with Mr. Perfect for a brother. You know, the one that NEVER got into trouble! Brother Perfect never got grounded while I, on the other hand, spent much of my teenage years grounded to my room. And what do you do for hours alone in your room at that age? You think about creative ways to find more trouble or for it to find you.

Then because I was the only girl in the family, my father felt it was only natural to expect more from the only boy when it came to business. When we got out of high school, we both joined the family car rental and mini-storage business. It wasn't my father's fault for thinking that my brother would excel in business over me. Back then business was, for the most part, a man's world. Women were given secretarial jobs or were assistants to their male bosses. At the time, it wasn't commonplace to instill leadership confidence in women. Therefore, I was always trying to measure up to my father and my bother. I was determined to prove that I was worthy of my own independent success.

Dad always supported my independence, and even allowed me to buy in to the family business when I was just 19 years old. But I would spend years trying to build up enough confidence to leave the family business and prove to him that I could make it on my own.

When I turned 30, the timing was right, and I looked for the first opportunity to move away from the family business. The big push for me came when my dad told me he wanted to start a port-a-potty rental business. Now I could just see what would happen next. Dad would throw the business in my lap to run, as he did with many of his entrepreneurial ventures, and when the employees didn't show up on the weekend to clean out those toilets—guess who would get the job? It was time for me to go!

Having never applied for a job in my life, and having never attended a day in college, did not hold me back from feeling confident that I could make it on my own. Sure, it was scary, but my determination drove me to action. I already had discovered that if you're not taking risks that scare you from time to time, you also are not moving yourself forward. Therefore, I was determined to prove to the men in my life that I could run my own company. I was determined that no lack of knowledge, skill, or confidence was going to stop me. One problem, though, was I had no idea what I was going to do. I knew that I could sell just about anything. After all, I was taught by one of the best car salespeople on the planet—my dad. So if I could run a business that sold something, I knew I'd be okay.

I waited for the first opportunity in sales that came my way. That opportunity was to buy a ladies retail apparel store. It sounded fun and exciting to me but there were numerous obstacles and challenges I needed to overcome to make it work.

First, the store had never turned a profit in its six years of existence; and second, I had never worked a day in retail. What was I going to do with a retail store? I didn't know the answer to that yet, but I did know that I needed a change; and I believed that for some reason, this opportunity was the one for me.

A lot of people told me I was crazy. Sound familiar?

Negative comments flew at me from every angle: "I don't know how you think you are going to make it work." "You don't have any experience." "Why would you leave a career that pays you well to do something you don't know anything about?" "There are so many people that would dream of having your great paying job and company benefits. Why would you leave?

Are you crazy?" "How do you think you are going to get a bank loan and make any money out of a losing business?" "If you want to make it work, you had better make it more than a hobby."

You may have had to listen to people who doubted your abilities when you began your sales career too. You may have heard something like this: "Hey, what on earth makes you think you're a salesperson? You've never sold anything in your life!"

When I took the time to think about some of my own negative comments, some actually made sense. Then along with hearing those comments, came the fear of the unknown and the fear of failure. I almost held back, but I was passionate about starting my own business, and even more determined to prove them wrong.

If you've received negative comments when trying something new, you easily can relate to these feelings. Yet negative comments are just words and other people's limited beliefs—not yours! Most people tell you that you're crazy or doubt your abilities simply because they couldn't do it themselves or because they want to hold you down from moving beyond them. Don't allow your dream stealers to take your dream away. Keep going, believe in yourself, and prove them wrong!

> *"The greatest pleasure in life is doing what*
> *people say you cannot do."*
> **WALTER BAGEHOT**

I used all of the confidence I could muster to make the move. I fed my brain positive comments every day to wash away the negative ones. I spoke these words to myself every day to prepare for the big move: "Dad taught me a lot about business and gave me the gift of true entrepreneurial spirit. I've worked on developing a strong belief system, which in turn has built up my confidence. If I learned how to run all the businesses my dad started, I can do this too!" Although my dad had instilled independence in me and taught me a lot, he did not allow me to fly high enough. I didn't need the change to prove anything to anyone except to myself. Now I needed to soar on my own!

FIVE LESSONS LEARNED FROM A CAREER CHANGE

Lesson #1: Have an unstoppable belief system and the commitment to make it work. Take all of your frustration from negative comments and turn them into motivation. Motivation to make it work, no matter what! If you have a dream and lofty goals, you should allow no one to stop you. No matter how crazy they may seem. Remember, every innovative, gutsy, or unique idea is first thought of as a crazy idea.

Lesson #2: Many heads are better than one. Ask others for help and find a mentor. Shortly after making the move I discovered that a strong belief system and motivation were important, though they were not enough to get me past the next obstacle—learning the business, and learning it fast. Find support in salespeople who you admire, mentors who are skyrocketing, and people who already are exceeding their goals. Then simply ASK them for support and guidance.

Never underestimate the power of asking. Most of us don't ASK enough; and without asking, you will be limited to only what is handed to you. Get in the habit of asking for 50 percent more than you have right now. Even if you are a lousy asker, you'll probably get at least 25 percent more than you've got right now. I'm sure you want more.

Be aware that most highly successful people will reach out and help you faster than those who are still climbing the ladder to success. Many who are still climbing are not yet confident enough to share; successful people, on the other hand, already have made it to the top through others' support, so they understand it is their turn to give back and support others who also are enthusiastic and passionate about climbing fast.

Share your enthusiasm to be the best salesperson you can be, and then be a sponge when successful salespeople share their wealth of wisdom with you. Don't worry; you will repay the universe when you are at the top of your sales game by mentoring and supporting others too. What comes around goes around many times over.

If you are not willing to receive what is due you, you are robbing yourself and sabotaging your own sales success. Be open to receiving.

Lesson #3: Find your own luck through opportunities you seek out and act upon. You can create your own luck through opportunities that come your way. Sometimes it doesn't matter how crazy they may appear to be at the time. If you have true passion and commitment to make it work, and you continually seek more sales opportunities, any sale is possible.

You will never know if the opportunity is right unless you take a chance.

Lesson #4: Set big, crazy, and sometimes even unrealistic sales goals to stretch yourself. Back when I made this career change, I did not write out my goals; instead, I set up mental expectations and used strong visualization to move me along. At the time, if I had written out my goals, they would have held me back because they would have been too low. I knew so little about the business that I didn't really know what I was capable of.

I now believe that writing out specific goals that allow you to s-t-r-e-t-c-h will instill even more messages into your subconscious that will help pave your way to success. It's good to set big, crazy goals that stretch you. Every successful person was crazy at some point in their career. Give yourself permission to create some crazy and even unrealistic goals.

Lesson #5: When you do what you love and make a difference in people's lives, you never will have to work another day in your life. You have the privilege to share your products, services, and expertise to help others get what they want and/or need. You have an amazing job, allowing people to buy from you the things that will support and improve their lives in some way. You bring joy to others every day by giving them quality service and products at a fair price.

Selling is one of the most stimulating and rewarding careers that exists, and you do it like a pro. Your customers love you, and they make your sales job easy and enjoyable by staying loyal to you and referring others to enjoy the same experience of working with you.

COMPLETE SALES CONFIDENCE

Keep building your confidence by feeding your mind with positive affirmations. Your confidence guides you easily toward reaching, and exceeding, your goals. You can do anything if you think you can. People will respect you and have confidence in you too, because you are worthy of respect and confidence.

Accept that your subconscious mind is guiding, directing, and prospecting mentally and materially for you. Once you do that, your subconscious mind will automatically direct you toward complete sales confidence and wise decision making.

Without first examining the powerful subconscious suggestions that are currently operating in you, you will create behavior patterns that cause you to fail. Constructive, positive suggestions can release you from the mass of negative verbal conditioning that might otherwise distort your sales potential.

Constructive words and thoughts develop good habits. The lack of constructive words and thoughts makes it nearly impossible to create good habits.

"As is our confidence, so is our capacity."
WILLIAM HAZLITT

WHAT DO YOU SEE IN THE MIRROR?

You develop a positive mental attitude by being good at what you do, by being prepared, by understanding the realities of what it takes to succeed, and by having the self-discipline to base your actions on those realities.

Hence, the success cycle is self-perpetual: The more prepared a person is, the more confident they become; which translates into a natural positive mental attitude; which, in turn, builds self-confidence.

Others will view you the way you view yourself.

Based on what you believe to be true, how do you view yourself?

- Friendly and outgoing
- Positive and optimistic
- Open-minded and a life-long student
- Prepared and organized
- Helpful and supportive
- Generous and thoughtful
- Service-oriented and customer-focused
- Self-motivated and committed
- Brave and willing to take risks
- Focused and successful

What are your beliefs and habits? How do you feel about yourself? How confident are you in selling yourself? How well do you relate to others? How well do you support your own sales success?

The more confident you are, the more likely you are to change negative beliefs about yourself into positive ones.

When you have confidence in yourself, there is no such thing as "do it later." Don't focus on if you can succeed, focus only on knowing that you will succeed. Visualize yourself already being successful at a higher level.

List three areas that you can focus on to improve your self-vision now:

1. _____

2. _____

3. _____

When you visualize and play out your success in your mind before it happens, it appears easier when in reality. Visualization will allow you to feel more relaxed and confident because you already have moved outside the comfort zone of your mind.

What you form in your imagination is as real as any part of your body. The ideas and the thoughts are real, and one day will appear in your objective world if you are faithful to your mental image.

A mental movie played out in your head is the substance of things wished for and the evidence of things you cannot yet see. One area in which mental movie role playing appears especially useful is in selling real estate.

For example, if you have a house or property for sale, I suggest that you first become satisfied in your own mind that your price is right and fair to both you and the buyer. Now picture the sale completed, the check in your hand, give thanks for a successful day, and go off to sleep feeling the flow and ease of the mental movie created in your mind. Your mental movie will build up the confidence you need to trust yourself and trust the sale.

3

DEVELOP YOUR MENTAL COPING SKILLS

*"The flower that follows the sun does so
even on cloudy days."*
ROBERT LEIGHTON

Selling can be like taking a ride on an emotional roller coaster. Hold on and enjoy the thrill! You have chosen one of the most exciting careers there is, with unlimited possibilities for building income and wealth. Your career in sales will never be boring, will always be challenging, and will inspire you to grow and improve continuously.

There's nothing like making a sale to boost your confidence when you're in a slump.

Mental coping skills determine sales success or failure. Selling is a very emotional game. You are constantly tested and challenged. What drives you to reach your sales goals now, and how do you cope when being challenged at the sales game?

Successful salespeople see opportunities all around them. Do you see opportunity? If you seek out more opportunities, more will appear. Understand that when you take action quickly and move forward, more opportunities appear at your doorstep.

It is also important to understand that you will constantly be emotionally challenged, because every customer and every sales situation is unique. At times you will struggle with internal thoughts and feelings that will frustrate and challenge you. That is why it is so important to develop your mental coping skills to get through the hard times too.

For example, the average golfer spends about 86 percent of his time doing nothing but wrestling with his thoughts and emotions, feeling one way or another about what is taking place, feeling exhilaration or anger, struggling to keep focused, and worrying about what's happened or what's up ahead.

It only stands to reason that if 86 percent of the time spent playing the game is dominated by thought and emotion, not physical action, then 86 percent of the success/failure determination is due to management of thoughts and emotions, not swing mechanics or putting prowess.

How do you develop mental coping skills? Again, you start with observation. All salespeople produce thoughts in their minds that are not consistently supportive to their sales income, wealth, and happiness. As you identify your own damaging thoughts, you can begin to consciously replace those nonempowering thoughts with empowering ones.

Move away from the self-defeating mental habits of the past. What is holding you back from seeking out more sales opportunities? Everyone has the opportunity to be successful and wealthy. You deserve the best! You deserve to be successful, and to create an unlimited stream of sales income that flows to you easily and freely.

MOTIVATION IS THE DRIVING FORCE

Sales motivation is a primary factor in your sales success. The people who do the best in sales have strong internal drives and sales motivation. They internally believe they are doing the right thing. Look at this in contrast with a person who is externally motivated. This person gets their sales motivation by the strokes they receive from others. Instead, external surroundings motivate them.

Salespeople who create their own internal sales motivation tend to do best in the sales profession. Why? Because sales is a very emotional game! Salespeople are constantly being pulled in different directions with demands for their time and attention. So when you are internally directed, you have the confidence to trust your gut, your intuition, and to make the most use of your time. Motivated people learn how to prioritize their time and stay on track of their goals.

On the other hand, salespeople who use external direction to get their sales motivation often find themselves confused, unorganized, and overwhelmed. This blurs their focus and limits their success. They often question what others think they should do instead of trusting their own confidence and instincts to make their own decisions. Fears, doubts, and anxieties plague most sales professionals. Questioning and doubting cause emotional turmoil for the externally motivated salesperson.

If you want to be a highly paid, peak performance professional, you should understand this. You cannot wait for someone else to "motivate" you. You must create your own self-motivation.

Are you one of those people who get more motivation from external sources? If so, I suggest that you spend more time thinking about successful outcomes of your endeavors. Keep an open mind and trust yourself, even if you have no idea how to handle the situation. Simply believe that it is possible, and trust that you have the common sense to figure it out on your own. Do more of what already works for you. Set aside time to daydream about the time you aimed high and achieved your goal.

The more self-motivated you become, the more likely you will be to overcome fears, doubts, and challenges. The more fears, doubts, and challenges you overcome in your mind, the more empowered you will become. As you become more empowered, you create an amazing sense of pride that gives you the ability to overcome adversity and enjoy the exhilaration of success.

Opportunities are everywhere! They are only limited by your mind-set and your motivation!

Developing Mental Coping Skills

When I was writing this book, I asked Marcia Reynolds, author of *Outsmart Your Brain!*, for her insight into how best to develop mental coping skills when your sales are down.

This is what she had to say:

How do you maintain a positive attitude in tough times? If you make the following activities into habits, you may find your road offers a much smoother ride.

First . . .

Keep the big picture in mind. Have a vision of what you want your life to look like five years from now. Daily setbacks become minor obstacles when you have a clear, desirable destination in mind.

Second . . .

Reframe what you hear and see. Perception is the meaning you assign to events. We tend to focus on the worst possible outcome instead of searching for the alternative path. When you buy a red car, you see many red cars on the road. Similarly, if you keep looking for the opportunities and hold on to your faith that everything will work out (it always does), then you will see many options and find assistance along the way.

Third . . .

Remain focused. There is plenty of noise from the news, your friends, your family, and your paranoid brain that can distract you from your goals. Keep your payoff in mind. Pin up photos and pictures from magazines that represent your values and your dreams in your office and your home, where you will see them daily. When you get discouraged or afraid, smile at one of your pictures for inspiration. It feels great when you prove the cynics wrong.

Fourth. . .

Allow yourself to express emotion. Admit when you are scared. Then ask yourself what the worst is that can happen. Generally, you can live and rebuild from the worst, as unlikely as it is to happen. Admit to being discouraged. Then ask yourself what it will take to muster the energy to move on. Feeling emotions means you're alive. Channeling your emotions into positive results means you are courageous.

Fifth. . .

Believe. Watch movies and read stories about people who have overcome challenges. Recently I watched the movie *The Rookie.* My heart inflated with hope for my own big dreams to come true.

Tough times are a fact of life. How you handle them is up to you. Cycles are also a fact of life, so wake up every day knowing that the upturn will come. The one constant in this wave can be you. Make success a habit, and you'll stay in high gear no matter what.

The brain is designed to protect us, not to make us successful and happy. It takes special skills to outsmart the operation of our brains and truly act by conscious choice.

To learn more about Marcia's book *Outsmart Your Brain!*, her presentations, and/or coaching, visit her Web site at *http://www.outsmartyourbrain.com.*

POSITIVE ATTITUDES GET POSITIVE RESULTS; NEGATIVE ATTITUDES END IN FAILURE

Positive thinking is essential. Positive thoughts move you away from fearful thoughts. You already are acting positive by taking the time to read this book. Although you always hope and try your best, sometimes you will get the worst instead, so prepare your mind. Anytime I am faced with a difficult challenge, I think, "What is the worst possible thing that could happen, and how can I deal with it?" Once I've thought about the challenge in my mind and brainstormed positive ways to deal with it, my belief allows me to move beyond it. This mental process has helped me through a lot of difficult situations in life. Your own positive brainstorming sessions will allow you to do the same. Your thoughts and beliefs also will empower you with positive mind-set skills that will allow you to overcome roadblocks at the same time.

Anticipating and mentally preparing for short-term setbacks have the positive effect of ridding the impact of that obstacle to hold you back. This, in turn, paves the path toward long-term success. Prepared, you should go into every situation believing that you will make the sale, while at the same time preparing yourself for if you don't make the sale.

When you are faced with a difficult decision, or when you fail to see the solution to your problem, begin at once to think constructively about it. When you can brainstorm positive outcomes from challenges, you can move past any obstacle that comes your way. When you come up with a negative thought or find yourself in a negative mood, write it down on a slip of paper, wad the paper up, and drop it into the wastebasket. Now it's gone.

> *"The happiness of your life depends on the quality of your thoughts."*
> **MARCUS AURELIUS ANTONINUS**

Some of us have more optimistic personalities than others; yet, we all need to work on ourselves to be the best we can be. You can become more positive by taking the time to indulge yourself in the pleasure of positive thoughts several times each day. Be thankful for what you already have every day. The stronger your positive feelings become, the more motivated you are to aim at exceeding your sales goals.

Sorry to say it, but many salespeople are negative. The majority of salespeople don't expect to close a sale. They've been rejected so many times that they're actually surprised when they succeed.

Be alert for unproductive self-talk, such as "If it wasn't for bad luck, I wouldn't have any luck at all," "A day late and a dollar short, that's just the way I am," or "I've never been able to sell to this kind of a tough prospect—I guess today won't be any different."

Don't ever allow negative self-talk or rejection to stop you. You either have a product or service someone wants to buy from you, or you don't; there is no reason to take it personally. Don't waste your valuable time with people who are not interested. Move on to the next prospect. There are plenty to go around.

When making sales calls to prospective customers, don't assume the sale on your first visit. Don't expect that your prospective customer is eagerly anticipating your visit; oftentimes, that is not the case. Instead, stay positive and hopeful that this prospect has a real interest and need in what you have to offer. Don't worry or think negative thoughts about your skills and opportunities. Don't worry about the thing you fear the most—losing the sale. This is time for you to make a connection, discover if there is an interest, introduce yourself and get to know them, discover their needs, and build trust. Sure you want to make the sale, but patience and relationship building must come first.

Blaming the weather, the economy, customers, or competitors—these are simply excuses that allow negative salespeople to become victims. So why would anyone want to be a victim and sabotage their own success? Because this negative self-talk allows them to be set free of their responsibility. Salespeople often use negative thoughts to justify and rationalize their poor sales results.

"It couldn't be me. It must be something else. Right?" Wrong! If your sales are down, you had better take a close look in the mirror, because most of the time the root of poor sales results comes directly from you instead of outside influences. When you find this happening, stop to examine your thoughts, mind-set, and belief system; and begin instantly to take responsibility to stay positive and focused. You have the power to move beyond any sales obstacle. You have the power to turn your sales around by ridding yourself of self-doubt and negative thoughts. Adjust your thinking and get selling!

Your thinking determines your decisions, and your decisions determine your actions, which eventually determine your sales failure or success.

Your perceptions and/or beliefs about sales as a career can make or break your success. Often, it is simply the perception people have about selling that makes them feel uncomfortable with selling as their career, even when they have proven their success over and over again.

Never allow your mind to doubt your sales abilities. Don't allow self-doubt to rob you of one of the most rewarding careers—a career in sales.

Unfortunately, my friend William robbed himself of an amazing career in sales because of a lack of confidence and self-doubt. Yet, he had no reason to doubt himself. He was outgoing, charming, and good looking, and he enjoyed helping other people. He proved that he was a successful salesperson by reaping the rewards of huge sales commission checks when he was selling used cars and campers. His income from sales far exceeded any career he had ever had, and he enjoyed working with the other salespeople on his team. But he didn't like to sell. In fact, he disliked it so much that he left his high-paying sales job for a low-paying job that made him feel more empowered. Was he just opting for a comfort level that gave him a false sense of empowerment? I'm not sure.

Although he had already proven his success, he allowed his lack of sales confidence and personal beliefs to convince him that selling was not the career for him. When he did poorly, he feared his sales job was too hard and his income too uncertain.

When he did well, he quickly went through his money instead of saving it—as if he was not worthy of the income his sales career produced for him.

"Selling is just not for me. I'm not comfortable with it," he said. Now, what is not YOU about meeting new people, making new friends, selling people products they love, having fun while doing it, and getting a big paycheck too?

Do NOT tolerate for a minute the idea that you are prohibited from any achievement by the absence of inborn talent or ability. This is a huge lie, and one of the saddest sales excuses that exists.

"When things are steep, remember to stay levelheaded."
HORACE

POSITIVE ACTION STEPS TO RID YOURSELF OF NEGATIVE FORCES

For the next seven days, I challenge you to completely avoid and rid yourself of negative thoughts. During this mind-training exercise, I suggest that you wear a wide rubber band on your wrist to remind you to stay positive. When a negative thought comes to your mind, catch yourself and snap yourself out of sabotage mode. When you catch yourself complaining or going into negative thoughts and negative self-talk, pull the rubber band back and snap it. This snap on the wrist should jolt you back to reality quickly.

4

POSITIVELY FEARLESS
SELLING

*"The hesitation to initiate contact with prospective buyers on a
consistent daily basis is responsible for the failure of more
competent, motivated, capable salespeople than any other factor.
Nothing else even comes close."*
GEORGE W. DUDLEY

Letting go of any fears that
hold you back from contacting more prospective customers
will set you free and open you up to more sales opportunities
than ever before. When you let go of your fears, or act in spite
of them, your sales will skyrocket. Great salespeople put themselves at risk, no matter what their fears.

When you convince your subconscious mind that positively fearless selling is yours, and that it is always circulating
around you, you will inevitably have it.

Fear is a powerful restrictive force that can have a fundamental influence on salespeople. It stops them from doing what
they want to do, it forces them to do things they don't want to
do, and it hinders progress and prevents them from reaching
their sales goals. There is no need to live with fear; just because
you cannot see a solution doesn't mean there isn't one.

If, for example, you are full of fear about reaching your
sales goals, you are writing a blank check and attracting nega-

tive conditions to you. Your subconscious mind accepts your fear and negative statements as your request, and proceeds in its own way to bring obstacles, delays, and limitations. Remember that your subconscious multiplies and magnifies whatever you deposit in it; if you deposit lots of positive checks into your mind, they'll show up in your bank account too.

SELLING FEARLESSLY WITHOUT EXPERIENCE

While writing this book, I interviewed a lot of different types of salespeople in many different industries, many of whom were new to sales. When my friend Linda confided in me that she was scared to death when she started a new job as a Yellow Pages sales rep, I was shocked. She is outgoing, funny, and charming, and she has been speaking in front of large groups of people for years. I wondered how she could be afraid of selling. Linda told me that she was so uncomfortable selling her services in her own company that she went out and found a part-time job in sales that would push her past her fears and out of her comfort zone. She said, "If I can get myself cold calling on business owners and sell them on a product I know little about, then I can move past my fears of selling and become more successful in my own company."

Linda did not make an easy transition into her new sales position, but she was committed to give it a go. On day one she drove to her first prospect. When she arrived, her fear took over so strongly that she couldn't get out of the car. She told me that she sat in the parking lot for TWO HOURS before she gathered up enough courage to get out of her car. She didn't make the sale on her first attempt, but was committed to keep trying.

"Hey, the fear was so strong that I was just pitiful, but it got easier as time went by. The next day it took me only ONE HOUR, and by the end of two weeks I was out of my car and into the business within ten minutes. That day I made my first sale. Wow! I was on such a high after making that sale that I wondered why I ever allowed myself to be paralyzed by fear for so long."

There is no such thing as the right time to take action. Don't wait—go for it.

Don't hang on to your fear longer than necessary.

How could Linda have moved beyond her fear and taken action sooner?

She could have done her homework, and been prepared to move away from the belief that she didn't know much about the service she had to offer. She could have trusted herself, her outgoing personality, and her belief that her prospective clients needed Yellow Pages advertising to promote their businesses. If they were not open to advertising, she could have understood that there was another prospect who was interested around the next corner.

When you enter into a sales presentation trusting yourself, open to positive beliefs about what you have to offer, and are fully prepared, it does wonders for your self-confidence. Knowing that you know everything about your product, company, and competition backward and forward works miracles in elevating your self-esteem and your sales.

The only way to be assured of this kind of comfort is by trusting yourself and by doing your homework in advance so that you're 100 percent certain you can handle any situation that might arise.

Often, when faced with a new problem, we act as if it was the first one. We tend to act as if past successes never happened. And when that happens, we stop believing in our abilities. We worry instead of concentrating on finding a solution. No matter how confident you are, it is only natural to have feelings like this from time to time.

It is possible to rid yourself of fear as long as you are determined to work on it. You weren't born with fear. You acquired your fears from past beliefs, thoughts, and programming. Fear is an illusion, a thought, and thoughts can be changed. We all have different perceptions about what makes us afraid.

Last year I attended a personal growth workshop presented by Marshal Sylver, a world-class hypnotist. I found the event to be empowering, and enjoyed watching people respond when asked to do things that they were fearful of. He told us that by the end of the weekend we would all have an opportunity to eat fire. Now I can't say that eating fire ranked as one of my goals to achieve in my lifetime, but the idea of doing something in spite of fear did intrigue me.

It amazed me that with a room full of 300 people, nearly 80 percent walked to the stage to give it a try. Maybe they where all hypnotized, but I was fully aware of my senses and my fears.

I watched as a line of people took to the stage to go for it. They did it, and instant excitement and empowerment took them over. I had to give it a try. With my palms sweating and my heart pounding, I took the stage as Marshal grabbed my arm. I put my trust in him and let go of my fears. The next thing I knew, I had a flaming torch down my throat. Then, the next thing I knew, the flame was out and it was easier than I imagined it would be. By paying careful attention to directions and trusting that I could do it, I discovered there was nothing to fear but the fear of the unknown.

Most people succeeded in the same way. But some never even moved from their chairs, allowing the fear to paralyze them and keep them from trying. Others changed their minds as they approached the stage, or tried a couple of times to put the flame in their mouth and then gave up unsuccessfully. And only a couple of people burned their lips when they focused too much on the fear and less on the simple instructions. They spent so much time thinking that they could get burned—that they actually did get burned. Your mind works in powerful ways. It either works for you or burns you. Fear either moves you forward to take risks that empower your belief system, or it keeps you stuck in the uncomfortable zone of self-doubt.

RIDDING YOURSELF OF FEAR HABITS

Learn to harness the tremendous negative energy generated by your fears and turn it to your advantage. Be open to learning and trying new things. Be open to discovery before fear sets in.

Act in spite of fear—in spite of your discomfort. When you feel the fear and act in spite of it, you are overriding your past limited beliefs.

Fear is not just a problem. It's a habit.

Most people choose to set small goals first and don't stretch themselves with more gutsy goals. They are scared of failure, and they're even more fearful of success. Yet, the fear of failure itself creates the experience of failure.

Salespeople limit their success due to small thinking and/ or lack of focus on reaching their goals. Limited beliefs and lack of focus often stem from a feeling of not being worthy of success. Salespeople who believe that they are not skilled enough, knowledgeable enough, or important enough to be the highest achiever in their organization set themselves up for failure. They set themselves up to get burned.

Fear is a negative thought in your mind. Confidence is greater than fear.

FIVE WAYS TO BANISH FEAR FOREVER

Following are five ways to help you banish fear:

1. Believe in yourself, your abilities, and your expertise.
2. Associate with confident, positive, and successful people.

3. Stretch yourself outside of your comfort zone to build self-confidence.
4. Ask for help and support from others.
5. Be honest, supportive, and caring of others.

Stop accepting the false beliefs, opinions, and fears that sabotage your success. Once you rid yourself of fear, you will experience wisdom instead of ignorance, calm instead of stress, success instead of failure, and confidence instead of fear.

How do you sell without fear when you don't have the experience?

Joel Weldon, sales trainer and founder of SuccessComesin-Cans.com, shared his wisdom when I asked him this question: "Because almost every sales professional begins their career with little or no experience, what can a newbie do to be successful?

"I suggest that people who are new to sales should tell the truth with enthusiasm and excitement and use this as their selling benefit."

Joel shared an example of what a "newbie" might say:

> This is my first year in this position as a representative for _____. Because I don't have a lot of customers yet, I can devote a lot of my time, attention, and energy to you and your situation, to ensure you get the service you want. Here's what you can expect: First, you'll see me again as soon as you _____ (take delivery or use the product for a week or get the paperwork). After that you'll be able to call me with any questions you have. I promise you, because I'm new, I will check with my wonderful support team that has more than 163 years of experience before I get you the answer! It's nice knowing I'm not too busy to service you, isn't it?

PROMOTE YOUR INEXPERIENCE AND MAKE IT A SELLING BENEFIT! LETTING GO OF THE FEAR OF FAILING

"Courage is the mastery of fear–not absence of it."
MARK TWAIN

Hopefully you make a mistake now and again, because failure can actually be good for your sales career. If you haven't made any mistakes for a while, you may be playing it too close to your comfort zone and not stretching yourself far enough or fast enough to achieve high-level goals. To aim high, you must accept some of the risks that go along with learning something new.

Although risks come with the acceptance that you will make some mistakes along your journey, you will want to avoid making costly mistakes or making the same mistake over and over again. Use good common business sense. Every business and every sales career has its share of challenges. You constantly will be tested in business as new challenges arise or as your business grows and expands.

You always will be challenged with new areas of your business that stretch you past your current abilities and expertise. It may be a big sale, the start of a new job or business, a new opportunity, or an extremely difficult challenge, yet all challenges will help you learn more about your business and help you build your self-esteem at the same time.

Renee Walkup, president and founder of SalesPeak.com, says that, when it comes to moving past the fear of selling, "people who have experienced the proverbial pushy salespeople in their lives are often fearful of becoming one of them, or are suffering from a primal fear of rejection. The reality is that professional salespeople are highly regarded, can always get a good job, and earn great money. Anyone who wants to get over his or her fear of selling needs to begin to think like a highly trained professional who is performing a service using advanced communication skills. Companies need professional salespeople because buyers are looking for advanced expertise that professional salespeople offer."

Think of yourself as an EXPERT instead of a salesperson. Everyone wants to deal with the EXPERT (the person in the know). As you master the art of communicating your expertise you move further away from the fear of rejection. Experts understand the tremendous value they offer their prospects. They don't allow rejection to get in the way of communicating their service with confidence.

LEARN FROM YOUR *MISTAKES* AND MOVE ON

Actually, I don't even like the word mistake. I believe that mistakes are simply challenges in disguise. Realistically, most of us don't get it right the first time around. Successful salespeople make mistakes all the time, but the only difference is that most of their failures go unnoticed because they don't give up and just keep on going.

Successful people make it look easy. It's easy looking in from the outside. We don't often notice or acknowledge their failures. Successful people evaluate their failures, come up with new solutions to the challenge, and try again—this time more educated than the first. Successful people don't allow the fear of failure to stop them from achieving and exceeding their goals.

If you study the failure and challenges of business, you will discover the ultimate success secrets of any enterprise. These are the key lessons an organization learns as it grows, expands, and competes in a changing marketplace.

If you want to create success, study all the failures. Most highly successful people were not successful from the beginning. They had to struggle a little or a lot to reach their peak potential. Walt Disney was actually fired from his first job because he was told that he was not creative enough. Not creative enough? Luckily, he believed in his own innovative ideas.

We all have a tendency to focus on success and fear failure when things don't go as planned. Don't be too hard on yourself if you feel that you are making too many mistakes to make it to the top. Hang in there and be patient. Once you overcome the challenge, you won't have to do it again.

With each failure you overcome, you also become positively fearless!

Success takes time, just as it takes time for you to adjust to and learn new skills. Be aware, however, that mistakes will continue to happen even after you've reached your highest level of success. You continually need to be learning something new to stay innovative and cutting edge. So when you think you have it all figured out and have made all the mistakes you need to, something new will challenge you again and test your confidence.

I've been an entrepreneur all of my adult life and I'm still making mistakes. I plan on making more of them. People always learn more from their mistakes than from their successes. Making mistakes, turning them into challenges, and then overcoming these obstacles in business are all extremely rewarding. There is nothing that can challenge, motivate, build confidence, and make you positively fearless faster than overcoming difficult challenges.

Mistakes and challenges are going to occur anyway, so the sooner you learn from them, the sooner you will become more successful in whatever you do. We tend to reach conclusions about success, but until success is compared with failures, you don't truly understand the whole story of how business works.

WHY DON'T THEY TEACH FAILURE IN SCHOOL?

Why do you suppose stories about failures tend to disappear from business education curriculum? While information about sales failures is often scarce or ignored completely, failure is inevitable. On the other hand, information about successful salespeople and their companies' success strategies is in generous supply.

Salespeople who pursue unsuccessful strategies either change their business strategies or they find another job. A successful company is described as having used visionary management and innovative selling and marketing strategies, while a failing business is accused of having poor business management and overall bad business skills. So why don't we teach future sales executives and entrepreneurs more about failure? Wouldn't that save us a ton of money from mistakes that could have been avoided in the first place?

Can you imagine telling your banker to add an additional $20,000 to your loan for all the mistakes that you plan to make in your new business venture? They would think you were crazy. Yet that is exactly what is going to happen when anyone develops a new business.

You simply must make some mistakes in order to see what works and does not work, and to test new ways of attracting more customers. It is necessary to make mistakes as any business grows. The reason why franchises have a larger success rate than independent company start-ups is because they already have made many of the mistakes and they have systemized the business to avoid them in the future. For the most part, franchises come with proven success systems that were created out of learning from past mistakes. Think of yourself as a franchise and systemize your selling strategies to work for you the same way.

*"I shall try to correct errors when shown to be errors,
and I shall adopt new views so fast as they
shall appear to be true views."*
ABRAHAM LINCOLN

SUCCEEDING FROM FAILURES

Joe Bonura, president of Bonura.com, works with businesses that want to increase sales and improve customer service. When it comes to succeeding from failures, Joe says, "We learn to walk by falling down; we learn to ride a bike by falling off. I have learned more from my failures in selling than I have learned from my successes. When I fail, it is like being hit on the head with a two-by-four—it gets my attention. It gives me an opportunity to focus on what caused me to fail, to learn from it, to do something about it, and then to move on."

In Joe's book *Throw the Rabbit: The Ultimate Approach to Three-Dimensional Selling*, he writes about the experience of his very first sales call. The media company Joe worked for was running an Easter promotion. With a 13-week schedule, the client received a six-foot stuffed Easter rabbit to give away. Joe walked into one prospect's place of business with the six-foot rabbit under his arm. He was so nervous that he tripped and fell; the rabbit flew into the air and landed in one of six garbage cans lined up against the wall. The garbage can fell over, knocking over the other five. Joe was down on one knee wishing he had never made the call, when he looked up into the smiling face of the prospect. The prospect said, "Well, that is the best attention-getting step I have ever seen in selling." Joe walked out with a 13-week contract, and a new concept that has made a lot of money for him in his sales career. And, the client got to keep the rabbit.

Find a way to throw the rabbit when making sales calls. Throwing the rabbit means setting yourself apart from the competition. It means standing out from the crowd.

Learn from your failures by focusing on lessons learned and not on your ego.

> *"Admire those who attempt great things, even if they fail."*
> **SENECA**

Before you can sell your product to somebody else, you must be 100 percent sold on it yourself. When you are sold on your products and come from a place of service instead of your own self-serving needs, you move away from fear.

When you believe so strongly in the value you provide to your customers, and care more about their needs than receiving large commission checks, you move away from the need to be in control and away from fear.

Place the customer's needs above the sale, and learn to give them value instead of discounts. Don't be the typical salesperson who is just hunting down another sale.

> *"Do the thing you are afraid to do, and the death of fear*
> *is certain."*
> **RALPH WALDO EMERSON**

Part Two

FIRED UP FOR SALES SUCCESS

5

THE JOY OF SELLING YOU TO THE NEW CUSTOMER

"Happiness is a butterfly, which . . . if you will sit down quietly, may alight upon you."
NATHANIEL HAWTHORNE

Much of what we have been taught about traditional selling no longer applies to today's customer. Why? Because the world around us has changed, customers have changed, and the marketplace has changed.

Today's customers are savvy and have learned how to service and sell to themselves without salespeople. They have a multitude of choices of how and what to buy, and also have the opportunity to find and buy anything they want around the clock on the Internet. They either can choose to buy alone and service themselves or they can seek out a sales professional to support their needs. So do today's customers want to deal with salespeople? While they don't need salespeople to be SOLD on what they want to BUY, they often do want to work directly with a salesperson who can assist them, service them, and educate them. Therefore, they need YOU!

The top salespeople develop comprehensive product knowledge. They not only know their business, but also the business of their customers. They develop remarkable insight and understanding of human nature and behavior. The best salespeople solve problems for their customers.

Professional salespeople help, support, and share knowledge with their customers. You always can assist customers in making a buying decision, but you can't SELL them something they don't want to BUY. Have you ever heard someone say, "Hey, look at what this salesperson SOLD me"? We all enjoy talking about things that we BUY, but never about what someone SOLD us.

When you get right down to it, good salespeople don't sell, so much as HELP. They pass along important information and ask customers to buy once they've demonstrated clearly how their product or service will help achieve the desired results or objectives. But, ultimately, the prospective customer makes the decision—not the salesperson. Therefore, it is up to you to know what it takes for your prospect to sell himself.

Do everything you can to make it clear that you have your customers' best interests in mind. Educate them on the benefits of your products and guide them in the buying decision process.

Some people require more motivation to make a buying decision. They want to buy, but get nervous about making the wrong decision and/or parting with their money. Be aware that it will be necessary to exert more guidance with this type of prospect.

REMOVE THE PRESSURE

No longer does the conventional high-pressure PITCH and CLOSE work. Okay, it might work on a few, but ineffective traditional sales pressure turns MOST customers off. Just as salespeople have their own selling styles, customers have their own buying styles as well. The only customers who are going to buy from a high-pressure salesperson are those few who have that type of buying style. Customers who don't have that buying style will run for the hills.

Your customers want you to sell to them in the way they want to buy. You will enjoy selling more than ever before when you move away from traditional sales habits, HIGH-PRESSURE sales PITCHES, and power CLOSES. Moving away from tradition will allow you to feel more relaxed and enjoy selling more.

The sale is not lost at the end of the traditional selling process . . . it is lost at the beginning.

You may have been selling the same way for years and making a good living at it, so why change? Because you are probably turning off more customers than you are aware of! Start paying more attention to your customers' reactions when you add pressure to the sale. Are they moving toward you or away from you? My guess is that they are moving away. This is good reason to begin to adapt to more effective sales strategies. Master the skills you need to embrace change. Move away from ineffective selling methods and toward more effective methods that allow you to sell with integrity. Come from a place of honesty and sincerity.

Being sincere is the easiest part of selling. It is simply a matter of caring about your customers and believing in what you sell. If you don't feel this way, my advice to you is to seek other employment or find a product to sell that you believe in.

The main reason why some people don't enjoy selling is because they simply have a negative feeling about selling. Yet to sell is to SERVE. If you are being asked to do things or have to do things to make sales that are in conflict with your personal integrity, it'll be impossible to be happy over the long haul. You must find a way to sell that you can feel good about.

"I never sell. Instead, I share," says marketing guru Joe Vitale, founder of MrFire.com.

"Think of the last time you saw a movie you loved so much you couldn't wait to tell others about it. When you told them, you were selling them on the movie. But you probably didn't think of it as selling. You were just excited and wanted to share. Well, that's how all selling should be. Share your joy for what you love in your product or service. As all good salespeople know, enthusiasm sells."

When you are fired up to sell with passion it is hard to keep from sharing what you have to offer with everyone you meet. It makes selling FUN! As you discover more ways to easily communicate your passion and value on a personalized level, the more your sales will skyrocket.

FIVE OF THE BIGGEST PITFALLS ASSOCIATED WITH TRADITIONAL SELLING

1. The approach is confrontational. When a customer feels confrontation, they often feel insulted, provoked, and challenged. These feelings would make anyone retreat verses being open, friendly, and approachable.

If you are too anxious to close the sale and/or working like crazy to get your prospect to see your point of view, you will only decrease your odds of closing. Selling is not about getting people to see your point of view. It is about allowing yourself to see other people's points of view.

The poor image people have about salespeople doesn't have to be the one they have about you. Remember that you're both on the same team, and both the seller and the buyer WIN. Your prospective customer must like you and believe in you. If not, there is no reason for someone to buy from you instead of someone else.

2. The customer feels pressured. When customers feel pressure, they feel that demands are being placed on them. High-pressure selling makes customers feel as if they are being has-sled. Pressure violates a customer's trust when the salesperson doesn't show respect for his or her ideas and opinions.

Customers don't want to be forced to stand up to pres-sure—and why should they? They don't want to have to stand up for themselves and argue with a salesperson either. Any salesperson trying to win an argument over a customer or pressuring a customer into buying will always lose out.

Creating demand and force doesn't work. Instead be pa-tient, respectful, and understanding. When you're able to turn pressure around, it becomes your advantage because you be-come elevated to a level far above your competition. When you truly want to serve your customers, they know it, and you'll overcome sales resistance.

3. Customers run from aggressive sales talk. Forceful, an-tagonistic sales talk is destructive. The number one complaint I hear about salespeople is that many of them are too pushy. Customers don't reward aggressive, obnoxious behavior. When salespeople are aggressive, their only goal is to talk, talk, talk and to share only what is important to them—closing the sale—period. Aggressiveness speaks from a self-serving place and turns people off instantly.

There is a big difference between aggressive and assertive behavior. When salespeople are assertive, they believe whole-heartedly in the value and quality of their products and/or services. Successful salespeople are self-assured and self-confi-dent, but never allow their sales talk to overwhelm or push away prospects.

People don't like saying no, but they will say no when hit with uncompromising sales talk. Naturally, it is infinitely eas-ier to say yes than it is to say no. Selling is all about trust and truth. When customers believe and trust your sales talk, they respond with a yes.

Here's an easy way to get more yes responses. During your sales conversation simply smile and nod your head up and down at the same time. People will follow your lead. What is the single word that comes to your mind? Yes! It is hard to get a no reply with a smile and a positive nod.

4. Salespeople begin the chase. Selling in full pursuit of winning the sale will move you farther away from it. When customers retreat, ineffective salespeople push ahead harder and faster as if hunting down their prey.

Overpowering the customer rather than showing how you can help is a sure way for you to descend into the stereotypical "hard sell" that no one likes. Such behavior is a great way to lose sales.

Move away from this game by creating more warm leads that come to you first. Customers who come to you are ready to buy, and are motivated to enjoy the process of working with you.

5. Salespeople lose the sale with self-focused goals. From whom would you rather buy, someone who is focused on you and your needs or someone who is focused on his or her own self-serving needs and goals? These are easy questions for your customers to answer. Now ask yourself these questions: Do you see yourself as a beggar and a taker or as a highly skilled sales professional? Do you see yourself as self-serving of your own goals or a salesperson who is a customer-oriented problem solver?

The issue is not changing someone's mind, but rather it is conveying to the person exactly why and how you can help solve a pressing problem. And you have to see and understand that problem before you can hope to solve it.

"You sell something to someone providing they need and/ or want it. Otherwise, you don't sell it. When you know that what you are selling is not going to serve the prospect the way they want to be served (or are expecting to be served), you let them know, and suggest other options for them," says Bob Burg, author of *Endless Referrals* and *Winning without Intimidation,* and founder of Burg.com.

"I've found that salespeople who take that honorable approach set themselves up for lots more business down the line. This could be because their self-esteem in knowing they did the 'right thing' empowers them in the future to sell with much greater power. They also will build up such goodwill with that prospect that they'll probably receive referrals from that person for a very long time, and have such a good relationship within that person's network that they'll find lots of diamonds in those acres. Talk about building a 'know you, like you, and TRUST you relationship.' WOW!"

I've always instilled the concept and importance of being 100 percent honest with customers when educating my sales teams. When I was in the retail industry my sales team understood the value of honesty in business and they worked hard to keep it at the forefront of their minds at all times. They understood that if they lost one sale by being honest, that it would be returned to them many times over. The value of building trust and truth in a sales relationship will by far win you more sales and referrals in the long run. Honesty is always the best policy when it comes to building long-term relationships with your customers.

SELLING TO THE NEW CUSTOMER

"Nothing astonishes others so much as common sense and plain dealing."
RALPH WALDO EMERSON

The customer of the past often waited patiently and saved for high-ticket purchases, such as cars or furniture. The new customer has the opportunity to BUY NOW instead of waiting to make more money before having the financial means to do so. With credit becoming ever more readily available to your customers to purchase virtually anything, they are now able to live for today and pay later with little or no effort on their part. This makes the buying decision easier for your customers, and awards you more sales opportunities.

But just because you have more opportunity to sell under the right conditions, it is your responsibility to be more credible than ever before. In the past, customers were more trusting than they are today. Your new customers are more suspicious of authority in general; simply being told that something is the case fails to impress them. They want to be given concrete evidence that things are as they are claimed to be before judging them either credible or unreliable.

Today's customers check labels, study content, compare prices, scrutinize promises, weigh their options, and ask pertinent questions. They are more active customers than those of the past. They are well-informed and independent versus the less-informed and involved customer of the past.

To win over today's customers, you must change the way you sell to fit their buying styles. You must prove that your products and/or services are credible, promote the benefits of purchasing them from you, and get into your customers' minds and their hearts.

There are seven ways to connect with the today's customers:

1. Move away from traditional selling methods that add pressure to the sale.
2. Become more customer-focused and service-oriented than ever before.
3. Discover their needs and wants first and foremost.
4. Serve their best interests—not yours.
5. Come from a place of trust, truth, and sincerity.
6. Offer solutions to their problems and become a master problem solver.
7. Allow them to BUY—when you SELL, people retreat.

Another way to connect to the new customer is to master the benefits you offer for your products and/or services. "The best way to become a supreme sales professional to the new customer is to know the benefits your offering provides backwards and forwards. Remember, customers buy benefits—what your products can do for them," says Eric Gelb, internationally-recognized copywriter and founder of PublishingGold.com.

For a number of years, Eric was national sales manager for a major equipment leasing company. Their product beat the competition hands down because the company offered excellent financing rates, no hidden costs or charges, and straightforward documentation. That offering typically cut the customer's leasing costs by 15 percent—a significant savings. This made the purchase decision relatively easy for those companies who were already leasing. Eric advises that to ensure success, you should be sure to organize your sales calls and presentations around the benefits.

What benefits do your products and services offer that will be tremendously valuable to your target market?

TAP INTO YOUR FEELINGS

"Mastering your own mental perspective is the fundamental and primary hurdle to overcome when selling. You must first recognize that it begins with your own thoughts and feelings. The next step is to decide to take control of those feelings," says Bill Brooks, an internationally known sales expert and founder of BillBrooks.com.

To take control, Bill suggests you follow these three primary steps:

1. Realize that you will never be any more successful than your self-image will allow you to be.
2. Realize that your self-image is directly connected to how you view selling. If you see it as a noble profession, you

will feel good about it and yourself. Face it, in our society we define who we are by what we do. It's that simple.

3. Only sell in ways that fuel the positive images of sales as a profession. Sell with integrity, honor, and dignity. Only sell people what they need and want—not what you want to sell them based on expediency, a quick commission, or an easy opportunity.

Are you coming from a place of excitement or a place of rushed anxiety?

Conventional ways of selling may have created habits within you that are hard to change. If you have been selling for a long time, you probably have been taught to take CONTROL, work on your PITCH, and GO FOR THE CLOSE. But all of these methods are self-serving, and for the most part, turn customers off.

I learned to sell by using many of these traditional selling strategies. It was the way that I sold for years because I did not know of a more effective way at the time.

Every time sales were off in my retail stores, I would go into rushed anxiety mode and put more pressure on myself by trying harder, pushing more, thinking only of the CLOSE, and thinking only of my self-serving goals! The more I added pressure to the sale, the less I sold.

My sales pressure penetrated my entire sales team and, in turn, their sales went down too. During those times I was coming from a self-serving place—a place of worry and stress—not a place of joy. I worried about paying my rent, my bills, and my employees' wages. Because I was focusing on my needs more than on my customers' needs, they could feel the pressure and often retreated. My self-imposed pressure and negative thoughts were sabotaging my confidence and my sales at the same time.

There is one kind of selling you must never do, and that is sell yourself short.

On the other hand, sales were always up when business was good because I took away my own pressure. It was easy and fun. I enjoyed selling when times were good, and I always sold more. So why didn't I change to a more relaxed way of selling if it was working and was more enjoyable? Because I was coming from a place of fear. I believed that if I relaxed and let up, my sales would drop off. Yet just the opposite was true.

Financial pressures can shrink one's self-image. On the other hand, prosperity and a feeling of prosperousness and independence feed on it and strengthen self-image. Self-image must be conditioned, strengthened, and prepared for the success you seek.

Are you moving toward your goals to help others or only to serve yourself?

I wish someone had taught me another way of selling years ago—a more relaxed, service-oriented, and effective way of selling. After embracing new beliefs and habits that made for more effective customer connections, I stopped sabotaging lost sales opportunities and my sales began to instantly skyrocket.

One's selling signals put out either positive or negative vibes, just as how you feel about your customer and their needs is telegraphed by the way you talk, stand, and walk. Believe me, although you might not think you're conveying signals to your prospects, you are. It's written all over your face. Is that signal a frown or a smile?

Visualize your customers' gratitude for the fine service you give them. What you visualize eventually becomes reality.

Are you coming from a place of service or a place of ego?

When a sales transformation happened for me, it formed a new sense of self-confidence that now allows me to feel more comfortable with selling and moved me away from ego-driven goals. I began to feel more relaxed and joyful about helping my clients invest in my services and products.

When you choose to come from a place of strong intentions to serve and enjoy your customers, you discover joyful rewards. Those rewards will come to you in the form of confidence, peace, money, benefits, repeat business, and referrals.

The most successful salespeople are positive, reliable, customer-focused, service-oriented, determined, persistent, hard-working, enthusiastic, and master communicators, and they consider themselves experts.

Are you coming from your heart or from fear and insecurity?

When you come from a place of fear, it is impossible to enjoy selling. You'll always want more, fear more, and worry more. If you are pushing for the sale out of the fear that something bad will happen if you don't push, you're coming from the wrong place.

When business is slow and you're feeling down, I recommend calling several of your satisfied customers for a brief chat. This call can serve a dual purpose. Perhaps you can pass on some new information that will benefit them. You also should inquire how they feel about the quality of service you offer. Then let them talk, and just listen.

JOYFUL SELF-PROMOTION

In the business world, when it comes to becoming successful, if you don't toot your own horn, I guarantee nobody will toot it for you. The world is not going to beat a path to your door to find you unless you tell them about what you have to offer.

The most successful salespeople promote themselves, their products, and/or their services effectively, with a strong conviction and commitment to help more prospective customers reap the benefits of what they sell. This is by no means a self-serving practice.

Only after writing my book *Confessions of Shameless Self Promoters* did I discover that most people felt differently than I did about self-promotion. It amazed me to discover that, on average, more than 85 percent of the people I surveyed in my audiences felt extremely uncomfortable with the concept of self-promotion—much less *shameless* self-promotion!

Most of the people in my audiences are salespeople so, therefore, it surprised me even more that they didn't self-promote. Many admitted to holding themselves back from self-promoting because it made them feel uncomfortable, even when they knew that they were sabotaging sales opportunities.

Most people who have an issue with self-promotion also have an issue with themselves and/or what they are selling. It often is difficult for them to imagine that other people would believe so strongly in their value that they would want to share it with everyone who comes their way in any way they can.

Are you underselling? Do you fear you will be perceived as too pushy, too salesy, rude, or aggressive? Salespeople undersell and hold back from asking for more business out of this fear of self-promotion.

Where did their uncomfortable feelings and beliefs about self-promotion come from? Many were programmed early on in life from their parents and/or teachers who told them that "it's not polite to talk about yourself. If you do, it will come across as pushy or rude, and you will appear to have a big ego." Your parents may have taught you that too, but they also probably said, "Go out in the world on your own and be highly successful."

Go out in the world and be successful—but don't promote yourself? Now doesn't that go against the grain of all sales and marketing success! How can you be successful if you don't seek out more ways to tell others about what you sell and how you can help them? You can't!

If you don't self-promote, you are holding yourself back from too many missed opportunities and the sales success that you deserve! You already know how to do it. In fact, you were self-promoting in grade school when you raised your hand to show the teacher you knew the answer.

Undeniably, there is unethical self-promotion. We've all witnessed it, and maybe even been turned off by it. Others who feel uncomfortable promoting themselves have a negative feeling about it because they have witnessed this type of ineffective self-promotion too often. But be aware that this is ineffective self-promotion—self-focused and ego driven.

> *"Egomania is a strange disease—it makes everyone sick accept the person who has it."*
> **ZIG ZIGLAR**

Egomania and ineffective self-promotion are not what I'm talking about here. What I do want you to understand is that you can and should self-promote ethically, regularly, and effectively to attract more customers to you.

Okay, but how do you promote shamelessly? First, let me share with you what the word shameless means in Debbie Allen's dictionary:

> shameless self-promotion: looking for opportunities everywhere to promote yourself in the service of others

Promote yourself and what you sell in the service of others! When you come from the belief that when you are self-promoting it is to help, support, and service others, there is NOTHING self-serving about it. When you promote from your heart and the passion to truly help others with the products and/or services you sell, you come from a place of caring.

To come from a place of service, caring, and joy, you MUST believe that what you have to sell is the best in the marketplace. You must be passionate about your products and/or services, and believe that yours are better than your competitors are. And you must believe that you would be doing prospective customers a DISSERVICE by not promoting what you have to offer them.

Do you have a discomfort ROBBING you of more sales success? Face up to it. Acknowledge it. Devise strategies to relieve it.

By NOT promoting yourself effectively, you ROB prospective customers of the opportunity of doing business with you. You ROB them of the positive experience of dealing with a salesperson who cares about their best interests and wants to offer them the best buying experience possible.

Doesn't this help you feel more comfortable with the concept of self-promotion? Or do you still need to work on your own beliefs more before you can sell yourself on the concept of promoting YOU? You have a choice: You either can change your beliefs and sell yourself on the concept, or you can sit back and take the crumbs that come your way. You must believe that you sell the number one product—YOU!

Would you rather have more sales and income, or more debt and fear that ROB you of the success you deserve? It's your choice. If you choose wisely, you will open up your mind to another way of thinking about self-promotion—an effective way to self-promote.

How can you be successful if you don't believe in yourself and what you have to offer to your customers? You can't! Therefore, the first step in successful self-promotion is to have a strong belief system. This positive belief has pulled me through many difficult times in my personal life and my professional life. When you have this belief, the universe will bring you many opportunities. Therefore, only good comes to you in even the most difficult of times. It is powerful and it really works!

Remember to look at self-promotion from this day forward as serving others instead of self-serving. Don't you want to help more and more people who could use your services and/

or products? You can't do that if you don't successfully self-promote and tell more people about what you do. Tell others why you are the expert and share success stories from your customers who love you. Your self-promotion, when done well, helps people get what they desire. When people get what they desire, they continue to support you and your sales success.

Next, you will need to add your own self-promotion STYLE. By adding your own UNIQUE style or fingerprint, magnificence, and essence to your self-promotion, you BRAND YOU in the customer's mind. This allows you to stand out in the crowd of other salespeople in your marketplace and joyfully rewards you.

How do you BRAND YOU? First, think about what makes you different from your competition. What makes you stand out and become memorable in your field of expertise? For example, because the title of my books in the Shameless series personally branded me, I'm now called "The Shameless Diva." I had no idea that I would ever be called "shameless" must less a "diva." But I'll gladly take the title, because it helps me to uniquely position my expertise with diva style.

Shameless is now a part of everything I do, including the license plate and the bumper sticker on my car. Shameless yes, but does it work at getting me noticed and support my unique individual style? And has it helped this somewhat modest girl promote what she has to offer in the service of others? Yes, you bet it has! And it will work for you too!

The more you can uniquely position your expertise, the more people you can help! No person is your superior. Everyone is unique. There's no one else in the world like me or like you.

Dare to be different and create you own selling style.

The reason it is so easy for me to promote my books, CDs, boot camps, and professional speaking business is because I love what I do. I feel so passionately about helping others. The products and services I offer have a proven track record and have helped thousands of people around the world become more successful and wealthy, and, in some cases, they have even created life-changing results. Therefore, out of my passion and joy for what I have to sell, I support others' success. How cool is that?

If you have the same type of passion and joy for what you sell, you will be doing a grave disservice to others if you hold yourself back from promoting YOU. After that, it would be your prospective customer's decision to either pass or decide to buy, and/or refer you to others.

Successful self-promoters don't ever give up! They keep going even after they have made big sales mistakes. They hit the wall, stand up, dust themselves off, and move in another direction. Most salespeople give up way too soon. In fact, there are some who show proven track records of success and have customers who love them who may still give up because their confidence does not support what they've already proven to be true. So they throw their hands up in the air and stick with the limited belief system that they can't make it work.

But you are not going to give up on losing out on missed sales opportunities by not promoting yourself effectively! Right?

Showcase your sales expertise. People simply are more respectful to salespeople who demonstrate expertise in their field.

FIVE WAYS TO PROMOTE YOUR EXPERTISE

Following are five ways to promote your expertise:

1. Develop a positive belief system by investing in YOU. Be a life-long learner! You'll be amazed at how many excellent tools are completely ignored by salespeople. Keep up your motivation and confidence at the same time.

Turn to motivational seminars, books, and CDs. Make a commitment to implement at least one new idea each month. Keep your eye on salespeople who best exemplify the characteristics you wish to strengthen.

2. Seek out and act upon more sales opportunities. Promote yourself everywhere. Even in elevators—where you have a captive audience. When you really start looking for opportunities, you will discover that there will be a steady, endless stream just waiting for you to grab hold of and act on.

3. Build referral alliances or enlist "shameless" fans who promote you back. Some salespeople have admitted to me that they don't feel comfortable asking for referrals or testimonials when someone gives them a compliment. If that is you, get over it right now. This is the perfect opportunity to allow your loyal customers to refer you and support your success.

4. Take your expertise to a higher level of success. Example: Salesperson versus expert. Create a sales journal of your successes to measure and support your results in becoming an expert within your industry. Promote your expertise to the media for free publicity by writing articles and/or sending out press releases that tie what you do to the news. Natural talent is not enough. You must have the discipline to practice, analyze, learn, and grow.

5. Act on some gutsy goals that move you outside of your comfort zone. You came into this world to succeed. And to succeed at a higher level, you must take risks from time to time. Trust that you will not be placed face-to-face with an opportunity or challenge too big for you to handle. Believe that when you trust to take risks, you are presented with the situation because you are ready for it.

Successful salespeople are master communicators and understand the art of presenting from a true belief that it will benefit their prospect. They can and will promote themselves and their products, services, and ideas with passion, enthusiasm, and joy. Remember: If you don't toot your own horn, you can't enjoy the music.

6

TRIGGER ENTHUSIASM FOR EVERY PROSPECT

"Nothing great was ever achieved without enthusiasm."
RALPH WALDO EMERSON

The key to your sales success is to raise your own energy and enthusiasm; when you do, people will automatically be attracted to you and what you have to offer.

Enthusiasm and energy attracts!

You have a tremendous responsibility to your organization to always be ON. When you step on to a sales floor or walk into a sales meeting, you are on stage. Just as an actor walks onto a stage, you need to be ON every time your audience is watching you. Your customers are your audience. They always can tell if you are ON or just acting the part. Your attitude, energy, and enthusiasm play out your results. Make every effort to be ON during every moment you actually communicate with your potential customers.

So how do you get ON when you're feeling OFF? If you find yourself in a slump, it's a pretty good bet that you put yourself there on your own. Therefore, you can move out of that slump on your own too.

Emotion is created in the sale by your enthusiasm for what it is you're selling. Enthusiasm is contagious and your positive emotion will be transformed to the prospect. Selling is and always will be a conveyance of feeling. If you can get the prospect to feel the same way about your product as you do, they'll buy it. Greater passion and enthusiasm leads to greater sales— it's that simple. You express your passion and enthusiasm by the intensity of your voice, your body language, and your facial expressions. Be aware of these things, and use them as another tool to create more sales.

Effective selling is about creating emotion and ownership in your customer's mind first.

How can you create energy, enthusiasm, and optimism as needed on demand? You create it by building vividly imagined, meaningful, exciting, and worthwhile goals. Before going to sleep at night, line up the resources, thoughts, ideas, know-how, and confidence you need. You have every reason and right to anticipate successful results.

The belief you have in your product, service, and pricing and in yourself is what creates enthusiasm. The deeper your belief, the more you believe that what you have is the very best, the greater and more genuine your enthusiasm. When you present yourself as relaxed, energetic, and confident, your prospects feel that security too. It enhances trust and makes decision making comfortable.

Motivate yourself to ACTION. Get moving and find something to get excited about every day. All motivation is really self-motivation. So get motivated! What motivates you? Are you motivated by reading self-help books, by attending a great seminar, or simply by calling a friend or family member who brings you back to reality?

I make it a habit to stay enthusiastic and optimistic most days; in fact, my friends often call me when they need a boost.

But I have my OFF days too, and that's when I call my mom for a supportive jolt to get back my enthusiasm for life. Calling her makes me realize how lucky I am to have her in my life, especially when many of my friends have lost their dear moms. She also is a supportive, nonjudgmental listener. We all need a person like that in our lives—someone you can trust to always turn your energy around and jolt you back to reality.

When I'm traveling to my next presentation, I can't afford to have an OFF day. It is my responsibility to have high energy and contagious enthusiasm every time I walk on stage for my next audience. It's your responsibility too, because your customers are expecting the best from you every day. Your customers don't want to hear about your problems. You are on stage to support, listen, and share with enthusiasm what you know about your products and services.

The show must go ON—it's your curtain call!

MAKE OPTIMISM A HABIT

Optimism is massively misunderstood. Most people believe incorrectly that being optimistic means always feeling cheerful, happy, and "positive," never acknowledging adversity, problems, or setbacks. This sets up an impossible standard. Certainly, no human can go through life having only positive experiences, just as no salesperson can go through life without experiencing setbacks.

Why develop optimism as a habit? Because negative habits of blaming undesirable experiences or outcomes actually can make you physically sick. Pessimistic feelings or a "poor me" attitude create the same ill behavior. On the other hand, when you develop the habit of optimistic thoughts and responses, you might not only enhance your emotional well-being, you also might enhance your physical health.

If you don't enjoy dealing with people and helping them to discover solutions to their problems, then selling is not for you. Your attitude determines your outcome every day in sales.

> *"Life is a mirror: If you frown at it, it frowns back; if you smile, it returns the greeting."*
> **WILLIAM MAKEPEACE THACKERAY**

Create "I CAN DO IT" optimism habits. You can be inspired and motivated to seek new opportunities, to correct your course, and to rise above any sales frustration. You make this choice. No one makes it for you. Follow these four steps to develop optimistic habits:

1. Care about something passionately and make it part of your everyday life. What inspires you, motivates you, and makes you happiest?
2. Get excited about what you are selling and share with sincere enthusiasm. Feel the joy and the difference you make by offering value to your customers.
3. Enjoy life to the max and create a life balance that brings you peace and tranquility. Relieve stress by spending time in nature or through daily meditation.
4. See life as a kid would see it. Keep on learning, growing, and enjoying.

CREATE ENTHUSIASTIC CUSTOMER CONNECTIONS

Knowledge builds your confidence, excitement, and enthusiasm!

Customers want salespeople who know their products and services extremely well. One of the number one reasons why buyers retreat from salespeople is that they waste the buyer's time by not knowing the answers to simple questions about their particular products or services. Get to know what you are selling inside and out. Have your answers prepared, and be ready to respond to any question or concern that a customer points out about what you are selling.

Show sincere interest in your customer's needs and/or concerns.

Customers want to deal with people who are interested in their needs, concerns, and wants first and foremost. They want to work with people who really LISTEN to their problems and/or interests. Salespeople who only care about making the sale and collecting their commission turn off customers quickly. When you are not sincere, it will show in your body language and the way you approach a sale, and customers will recognize your insecurity like a neon sign.

Return calls promptly.

Return calls as quickly as possible, especially when a problem or concern arises. Be prepared and organized so that you appear more professional and you don't waste your prospective customer's time. Your customers will lose trust in you if you don't return their calls promptly.

Follow up and follow through.

You showcase your reliability when you follow up and follow through with everything. This includes before, during, and after the sale. Salespeople who leave the work up to the customer fall short and discourage the customer when the customer has to do the follow-up.

Come through on all your promises.

When you promise a customer something, always deliver. Never promise anything you are not 110 percent sure that you can deliver. Don't tell a customer you will TRY and then not deliver. When you say "I'll try," what the customer is hearing is that YOU WILL. Make sure to communicate clearly on everything you plan to follow up with and everything you promise.

Become a master communicator.

The most successful people are those who are masters at communication. To do this, you must learn the skills of connecting with people. Every business is a people business, and salespeople who know how to connect with charisma, charm, and respect and through open communication always win people over.

ENTHUSIASM MOVED ME TOWARD SUCCESS

Enthusiasm can give you the energy you need to take action. It motivates everyone around you—your sales team, your organization, your customers, and your business associates. Enthusiasm often can carry you far beyond any talent or skill you may be lacking because enthusiasm is contagious. It shows that you are exciting and open to learning more. It is a sincere positive attitude flowing out of you. Others naturally gravitate to this kind of energy.

I purchased my first retail clothing store when I was 30 years old. Back then I had several years of sales knowledge behind me but no knowledge of the retail business. I had never worked a day in retail before buying the store. I quickly discovered that I loved it and that I wanted to make it my new career. But, I had to learn fast if I was going to turn the business around and start making an income from it. I needed a fast-track college of retail so to speak. The only people I knew that could help me learn the business fast were the sales reps who I built my trust in. "I'm basically clueless about retail but I have a thirst for knowledge and I'm passionately enthusiastic to learn anything you can share with me," I said.

One of my sales reps told me of a group of very successful retailers who met each month to share success strategies. He asked if I would be interested in attending if he could get my foot in the door. Yes! Yes! Yes! He called me a few days later and told me that the group had invited me to attend their next meeting and that he would go with me to make me feel more comfortable and to introduce all of them to me.

I remember my first meeting with them as if it was yesterday. Everyone in the group owned their own retail stores and also had been selling most of their lives. Everyone in the group had been hand selected due to their success in the business, in noncompetitive areas, and they all had from 15 to 30 years of experience as retail store owners. I, on the other hand, had only 6 months of experience.

Although I didn't know a thing about retail, I was pretty good at networking. Understanding that good networking is about giving and receiving equally, it made me feel bad that I didn't have any knowledge to share with this successful group.

The group was welcoming, and I felt like they had taken me under their wings and allowed me to fly along with them. Their high level of success and knowledge was intimidating and I didn't feel like I fit in, but I was not going to let my lack of confidence and fear keep me from learning everything they had to share. I wanted to be successful, and nothing was going to hold me back.

After just a few meetings, I noticed something that shocked me. The group always waited until I got into the meeting room and sat down before starting up. I discovered they needed my support too. I had something wonderful to share with them after all. I had the gift of enthusiasm, which many of them had lost along the way after many years in the business. It was contagious and they wanted to catch it and bring that energy back into their own businesses.

What I lacked in knowledge and skill I made up for with enthusiasm. I do believe that without it this "newbie" would never have been accepted into this prestigious group. From this association I also learned that if you truly want to be successful at something, you can't do it alone. You must align yourself with people who are smarter, more gifted, and more talented than you are.

This group of successful retailers felt my passion, commitment, excitement, and enthusiasm for making my business work. They were open and shared all their sales and marketing success strategies freely with me.

This knowledge allowed me to quickly open my second retail store within one year, and within three years I had grown my sales ten times over. I sincerely believe that my gift of enthusiasm opened the doors that made it possible for my rapid success.

After building my retail stores to a high level of success, I decided to sell them and move away from the cold weather in Indiana to sunny, warm Scottsdale, Arizona. Before leaving, I shared my mentors and this amazing group with the new owners and the group welcomed them with open arms. It was like handing the new owners the same gift I was given to learn the business. It was like a 24-karat gold platter of success handed to them.

Both of the new business owners came into the business in a similar situation that I had, having little or no experience in the retail industry. They needed all the help they could get!

The new owners attended a couple of meetings but soon their excitement and enthusiasm faded. When they stopped attending the meetings, I asked them why. One confessed that it scared her to attend the meetings because she was so afraid of public speaking that it terrified her to stand up and talk about her business in front of the group. The other told me that it interfered with her "bowling night." Well everyone has different priorities, but why would someone invest thousands of dollars in a business and then make bowling her priority? For her, it was a way of holding herself back from becoming too successful. Crazy, but it's true. Most people who want success still fear it and hold themselves back from achieving too much of it too soon.

It was hard for me to understand how anyone could have walked away from such amazing mentors. Both of the new owners showed passion and enthusiasm when they purchased the businesses, but they allowed fear to steal away their success.

They sabotaged their future. Within just two short years they had turned a highly successful business into a failing one. They then closed their doors forever and walked away broke.

Don't ever allow fear to hold you back from the success you deserve!

Ask yourself these important questions now before it's too late:

- Are you sabotaging your opportunities to be the best salesperson you can be?
- Are you sharing your passion, excitement, and enthusiasm to learn more?
- Are you going it alone or asking for help and support from successful people?
- Do you fear success or anything holding you back from being more successful?

You become who you surround yourself with. Are you hanging out with salespeople who allow you to learn and grow enthusiastically? Or are you hanging out with negative complainers just to be part of the crowd?

To be successful in sales you must find mentors who will help you to enthusiastically ingrain new thoughts and beliefs about yourself and what you are capable of.

If you want to discover what your worth and income will be this year, start by thinking about the top five people you hang around most (kids and family count too). Write down on a piece of paper how much they make annually. Now divide that number by five. This number is probably close to what you are currently making. Are you happy with that number or do you want more? One of the easiest and most effective ways to give yourself a raise is to start hanging out with successful salespeople who make more than you do. Listen, learn, and absorb their skills and success secrets enthusiastically.

"Analyze your life in terms of its environment. Are the things around you helping you toward success—or are they holding you back?"
W. CLEMENT STONE

LISTENING IS A FINE ART

Don't assume that because a salesperson has two ears that they know how to listen. This is FALSE! Most salespeople are so busy talking or thinking about the next thing they are going to say that they don't listen.

Studies have shown that we only hear about 50 percent of what is said, though I believe that percentage is higher for salespeople for the most part. Studies also have shown that recognition is the number one motivating factor for humans. Make your customer feel welcome, important, and that you are hanging on to every word they say. Make them feel as if they are your best and most important customer at that moment.

One of the easiest ways to distinguish a successful salesperson from an unsuccessful one is to watch for the one who is a better listener. Successful salespeople have learned the art and skill of listening to and interacting with their prospects. Unsuccessful and unskilled salespeople, on the other hand, do all the talking and rarely give their prospect a chance to get a word in edgewise.

Listening is a skill that requires patience and commitment to master.

Everybody loves a good listener. Customers buy from salespeople who listen and respond. Truly outstanding salespeople are excellent listeners. In fact, effective selling skills require two-way communication. To present your product or service convincingly, you must also have the ability to listen intently. You can't be listening if you're doing all the talking.

You should be listening 60 to 80 percent of the time.

When most people think about a sales presentation, they envision the salesperson doing all of the talking and the prospect doing all of the listening. This is WRONG! When a salesperson is talking, that means he or she is not listening and learning. Listening is the greater part of learning. Some salespeople go on and on, thinking they're being helpful. But, if that's you, stop right now, because you are not winning—you are losing sales. It's a shame, but many salespeople are so busy gabbing away that they fail to listen to buying signals. Not only do you miss important buying signals when you chat away, you also waste both your own time and your customer's time.

A salesperson who refuses to listen is also a salesperson who appears pushy and rude. As I discussed in Chapter 5, nothing turns off a new customer quicker than pushy or rude salespeople. Understand how your prospects might feel if you didn't give them the time or consideration of patiently listening to their needs and wants first. Most of us would not accept this inconsiderate and one-sided relationship in our personal lives, so why would we accept it from a complete stranger who wants to sell us something?

When you master the art and skill of listening, you show powerful self-confidence, patience, supportiveness, and control. One of the best ways to master the skill of listening is to become a good interviewer. Ask questions that will help you understand the other person's situation. Then concentrate on listening to how he or she responds. When you get really good at interviewing and asking questions of your prospects, you allow yourself time to step back from the sale at the same time. When you allow prospects to do most of the talking, you are able to take notes on their comments. You also have time to think about how you will best respond to them instead of blasting away useless one-way conversation.

Listening is the only way to target your product to the unique set of problems and concerns the prospect presents to you. By staying focused on the objective of helping the prospect, you build trust.

I know listening is a hard skill to learn, and most salespeople never master it. We all want to talk and tell more about our product or services—especially when we are overly enthusiastic or insecure about the sale. I'll be the first one to admit this sales skill is one of the hardest for me to nail down. Sometimes prospective customers perceive me actually to be overly enthu-siastic, and that has resulted in some lost sales. Yes, you actu-ally can be too enthusiastic, but only when you allow your mouth to take over your ears!

While I have a tendency to talk too much some of the time, I did figure out how to make talking pay for me—as a profes-sional speaker. It's my dream job. I get to talk, and I get paid well too.

Yet professional speakers also need to be professional salespeople. Everything we do has to do with selling ourselves, our services, our ideas, our products, etc. What I have discov-ered about professional speakers is that, for the most part, they are really lousy salespeople.

While professional speakers generally can sell their ser-vices okay, they often are terrible about selling their own prod-ucts, such as books or CDs, in the back of the room after they speak. Most are polished and confident on the platform, but once they get off the stage and go to the back of the room to sell their own creations, they BOMB!

The reason they fail to sell effectively is because most are not comfortable selling their own products out of fear of ap-pearing pushy and/or not believing in their products' value. So what do they do? They keep on talking as if they never got off the stage.

The reason I know this to be true is because I did it for years and sabotaged my own success. I always can judge the performance I had on stage by what I sell in the back of the room after my presentation. If I have any doubt about my per-formance or the value my products have to offer my audience, my sales BOMB because I don't know when to shut up.

Again, my mom comes to my rescue when I need help with my listening skills. When my mouth takes over my ears, Mom is quick to remind me and call me on it. With only two simple words she can get me to stop on a dime. Her words: "Zip it!"

Mom has added to that saying over the years, and it is now a quick lesson I share with my audiences. She says, "Zip it! Listen! Take it in . . . and go with the flow!" When I share this with my audiences, I ask them to stand up and actually act it out so they can program their brains to remember it when they need it most.

When you catch yourself in a sales situation and you just can't stop talking, even when you know it is killing the sale, remember my mom's words of wisdom:

Zip it! Listen! Take it in . . . and go with the flow!

When you ZIP IT and sincerely listen, you will uncover a wealth of knowledge that will allow you to easily direct the customer toward the purchase. You will uncover the customers' key needs, learn about their business, learn about them personally, and learn what their interests are. This not only helps to build instant rapport, it also makes your customer feel important, and people love people who make them feel important.

As a special bonus, if you go to SkyrocketingSalesBook.com and click on "FREE BOOK BONUSES," you will discover the *Secrets to Becoming a Master Communicator*.

FIVE SALES LESSONS LEARNED FROM THE GRAND BAZAAR

The World Famous Grand Bazaar in Istanbul, Turkey, is retail wonder. In fact, it should be considered as the Eighth Wonder of the World! With 5,000 vendors and centuries of success behind it, I learned some valuable sales lessons during my visit.

What made one small independent retailer stand out and outsell thousands of other much larger retailers in an overly competitive marketplace such as this?

That question was asked of me during my presentation to the Retail Institute of Turkey. What a great question, I thought. It really made me stop to think about how this one independent retailer kept our attention so well for more than two hours. Not only did he keep our attention in a small 5' × 5' booth, he also convinced us to BUY A LOT. Here are the five sales lessons I learned from him as I watched his amazing sales skills take over our wallets:

1. He greeted us with a friendly, relaxed, and inviting welcome. All of the other salespeople were hungry for business and practically jumped out to grab you as you walked by. The busier the Bazaar got in the afternoon, the more aggressive the salespeople became. This behavior turned us off and we quickly moved on.

2. He knew his inventory well and paid close attention to his customers' buying signals. When he saw us looking at rings, he quickly grabbed a case full of similar types of rings and then invited us into the booth to take a closer look. He carried a good selection of unique merchandise but not too many diverse products.

3. He triggered our emotions with the obligation factor. The salesperson offered us some tea. Tea is a BIG deal in Turkey! I don't think they could live without it and they definitely could not work without it. I thanked him but told him I didn't like tea. He replied with, 'Oh, you must try our special Apple Tea. You will like it.' Without leaving his small booth, he picked up the TEA HOT LINE. Within minutes we were being served a delightful warm tea in beautiful glass cups served from a large silver platter by the tea man. Brilliant! He had a captivated audience.

4. He took his time to really listen and to get to know us as friends. We were really enjoying our time as we all shared personal stories and experiences with one another. He spoke good English and was very warm and open. It was apparent that he truly cared about his customers and that he enjoyed his work. He was a great salesperson and used his sales skills and expertise wisely by building a relationship with us first.

5. He waited until we had exhausted our shopping experience before he packaged a special price. There was a lot of inventory in such a small space and it was unique to other jewelry merchants in the Bazaar. Because we had made a few small purchases before meeting him, we asked his prices on similar merchandise and he proved to us early on that his prices were fair or in most cases even less than other merchants. Fair pricing, bulk discounts, and great service made a great impression on us. As we continued to shop, he had his brother run to somewhere else in the Bazaar to have our rings and watches sized. I was so impressed that I just wanted to hang around and keep BUYING. The longer you can keep your customers around the more they will buy. It's that simple.

TRIGGER YOUR PROSPECTS' EMOTIONS

Most buying decisions are based on emotions. Your customers may tell you that they are buying out of logic, but much of the time, they are buying out of emotion. When our emotions are high enough, we form logical conclusions that trigger us to buy.

Think about it: We all want things we can't afford. Most of us want to own the house that we can't afford, the car we can't afford, or the furniture we can't afford, or take a vacation we can't afford. Our logical mind informs us that making such a purchase is not within our means, that we can't afford it, and that it doesn't even make logical sense. Yet, our emotions often take over our logic.

When emotions take over logic, we begin to search for more ways to own what we want, to own what we are most emotionally attached to. The more emotionally attached your customers become, the more likely they are to buy from you. Therefore, triggering your customers' emotions during the sales process is a powerful way to increase your sales.

Learn how to implement emotional psychological triggers in your sales message to create more emotion, enthusiasm, and excitement in your prospects.

Get into the minds and hearts of your customers and you will have them for life.

Seven Psychological Triggers That Motivate Customers to Buy

1. Trigger existing customers to buy more from you. Salespeople are at all times hunting down their next prospect, the next person to buy from them. This hunt is always set in high gear. I believe that salespeople, for the most part, spend way too much time hunting down new prospects than discovering ways to sell more to their existing customers. Sure, you must seek out new prospects all the time, but when you focus more on the customers who already trust and love you, your chances of increasing sales improve.

Think about your very best customers—those VIP customers who are loyal, refer you to others, and always purchase the high-ticket items. Got a few names in mind? You can't afford to lose even one of them. If you lost them, you also would be losing out on your biggest sales. So that being the case, what are you doing to generate more business from them? What are you doing to market to them more effectively and at a higher level than other prospects who don't buy as much? Most salespeople spend the same time, money, and effort on selling to their very best customers instead of investing more in them.

Trigger their emotions by learning more about them. Discover new ways of selling to them and servicing them. Go after your customers' mind share instead of hunting down more of the market share available to you.

Instead of expending energy on prospective customers who may never notice you, spend more time and energy on those who already trust you. You easily can increase your sales by 25 percent or more simply by focusing on doing more business with your existing customers.

2. Trigger your customers to return more often. Salespeople typically let additional sales opportunities slip right through their hands. How? They lose sales by NOT ASKING customers to return. And not only do they not ask them to return, they allow their customers to forget about them! Your customers are not going to return to buy from you again if you allow them to forget about you!

The number one reason why customers don't return to a place of business where they had a good experience is because they where not reminded to return.

With so much noise and competition in the marketplace, it's amazing anyone can stand out in a customer's mind these days. That is why you MUST stay in touch with your customers on a regular basis and trigger their emotions with more reasons to return.

You can give them more reasons to return when you create a membership program that relates to the products or services you sell. Customers love belonging to "a place" because it creates a feeling of comfort and consistency that we have learned to trust and expect. Smart companies create membership programs that give their customers more value and more reasons to return.

Your wallet may be full of membership cards for many different types of businesses; I know mine is. We all love to consume and return where we feel welcomed, invited, and often times, called by our names. Calling your customers by name when they walk through your door and remembering something personal about them is another powerful way to make an instant connection.

Trigger reminders often by direct mail about your organization and what you have to offer. How many times a year do you send out a direct mail piece to your customers to remind them of you? Eight times a year, 6 times a year, 3 times a year, or less? To stay in touch, you should be sending them a marketing piece in the mail at the very least 8 times a year, and I would suggest 10 to 12 times a year is even better.

Don't ever allow your customers to forget about you—rain mail on them!

Your direct mail marketing piece does not have to be elaborate nor does it have to make sale offers, but it must have some type of BENEFIT that triggers them into taking action. Postcards and greeting cards are both inexpensive marketing tools that can personalize your message and allow you to stand out. Note that the more personalized your message is, the more likely it is that your customers will respond.

Trigger their emotions by using mailers to promote your other products or services that you feel they would enjoy. Get them involved in your message and allow them to "buy into" additional offers.

Ask your customers to refer you to others more often. Offer them some type of referral reward program as a thank-you for sending business your way.

3. Trigger your customers with reasons why. Salespeople who inspire emotion in their customer's mind allow their customer to come to their own logical conclusion on why they should buy. Look at what you have to offer and how you promote it with new eyes—your customer's eyes. See, feel, and think like a prospective customer by stepping outside of yourself.

Often, we are too close to our own businesses to see the most obvious things that our customer sees. Discover the most powerful benefits and values from your sales message that connect with prospects on an emotional level. Build structure in your sales and marketing message to stay in touch with your customers often via e-mail, phone, and/or postal mail. Don't assume you know how they would like you to communicate with them. Ask them how they would best like you to connect, and then be sure to follow up with them.

4. Teach your customers how to consume. Teach your customers to support, refer, and stay loyal to you and your organization. When you can get your customers into a habit of doing business with you over and over again, you'll have them for life.

Some companies are so brilliant at developing programmed consumption in their customer's mind, that they actually "own" their business. Take Starbucks, for example. When we think of treating ourselves to a special cup of coffee, we think of Starbucks. They have branded themselves directly into consumers' minds around the world. That is an amazing feat considering that the first Starbucks opened its doors in the early 1970s with one small coffee shop based out of Seattle's Pike Place Market.

By the mid-1980s, founder Howard Schultz, a former plastics salesman, had opened more than 100 coffee houses and created nearly $60 million in annual sales. Today, Starbucks profits are five times greater than the industry average. Schultz had succeeded in crafting an authentic, new coffee-drinking experience. He triggered emotions in consumers by artfully re-creating the authentic look, feel, and smell of genuine Italian coffee houses. He created an atmosphere of relaxed self-indulgence that quickly related to the new consumer who wanted to unwind, meet friends, and savor the aroma of freshly brewed, personalized coffee choices.

> *"The companies that are lasting are those that are authentic. If people believe they share values with a company, they will stay loyal to a brand."*
> **HOWARD SCHULTZ, STARBUCKS**

5. Trigger your customers' emotions by answering objections up front. Most of the time when customers have a problem, salespeople take it personally and retreat. When customers call to discuss a problem or issue they are concerned about, salespeople either wait to return the call or don't return the call at all. That makes customers even more upset.

Did you know that most customers who bring up a concern are usually trying to tell you how to improve? Most customers likely wouldn't care if they didn't plan on continuing to do business with you. They want you to improve so that they feel good about coming back. So don't take it personally. Think of customers voicing their concerns as an opportunity for you to get better. When you think of it as a complaint, personal attack, or criticism, you'll most likely alienate the customer and lose them forever.

The best way to trigger their trust factor is to put obligations up front. Yes, come right out and tell them the answer to what they may be thinking instead of hoping they avoid bringing it up. Believe me, they already are thinking of it if you are.

For example, if your customer informs you that they believe the price is too high, you either can assume that they won't buy or you can agree with them and respond by informing them why. State something like this: "Oh, I can understand why you may think the price is rather high at first compared to similar types of items in other stores. Some of our other customers had that concern at first too, but when they discovered our amazing quality and long-lasting value, they were thrilled with their purchases. I know you will be too."

6. Trigger your customers by building curiosity, interest, and trust. Infomercials are brilliant at triggering emotions. If you want to learn how to trigger your prospect's emotions, you can learn a lot from watching infomercials.

Warning! Keep your credit cards hidden and pay close attention to how they pull you in with the curiosity factor. This may happen even when the offer appears outrageous or unbelievable.

Infomercials trigger your brain and emotions with most of the mind motivators I've mentioned here and then some. Infomercials sell you the hopes and dreams that fulfill most of what we all want more of—health, wealth, sex, and time.

- Watch as they demonstrate the many different uses and/ or benefits of the products.
- Feel yourself drawn in with the special free bonuses when you act now.
- Listen as they share amazing testimonials that build curiosity, interest, and trust.
- Be aware of how they overcome objection with four easy payments of just $X.
- See how they trigger you to take action with the fear of loss by not acting quickly.

There is good reason infomercial companies practice their science and magic of the mind in the middle of the night. This is the time when your subconscious mind (the nonjudgmental mind) is more likely to be acting from an almost hypnotic state. It makes us want to believe and trust what our conscious mind does not allow us to believe. The subconscious allows us all to believe even with a sliver of truth. We want to believe in any offer that will make us healthier, wealthier, sexier, or save us time.

My dad has purchased just about everything TV infomercials have to offer. In fact, he could start the first "Infomercial

Museum." Some of the things he has purchased haven't even been opened yet. He swears that someday he may need them, so he has never returned them. He even has shelves in his garage lined with all of his infomercial products on display. Lately, he really has been hooked on his new "Magic Bullet." He loves it so much that he uses it three times a day.

My family teases him a little about all the things he has purchased from TV, but we still love to hear about what works and what doesn't. Why? Because we're all curious!

7. Trigger your customers with demonstrations and freebies.

Demonstrations, try-before-you-buys, ethical bribes, and freebies are all brilliant marketing strategies that touch customers' emotions. Nothing works faster to get them to interact and respond to an offer.

There are many ways to trigger emotions with demonstrations. You'll know what works best for you, but here are a few examples that may get you brainstorming for new ideas.

Have you ever been to Costco, Sam's Club, or a similar type of retail warehouse on the weekend? If so, you have witnessed for yourself the mad feeding frenzy created at the food sample demonstrations.

During my last visit I had to wait for the oven timer to go off four times and kick two kids out of the way before I could grab my hot chocolate chip cookie off the tray. It was scary, like taking my life in my hands, but worth every bit of the risk!

The next thing I knew I was heading to the freezer section to get my own 50-pound tub of cookie dough! Why one single woman who lives alone with a 6-pound cat needs a 50-pound tub of cookie dough is beyond me. But I do know that emotions can trigger you to do weird things at times. Guilty as charged!

Once in a while I crave Krispy Kreme Donuts. If you've ever had one, you know why. When I have that special craving, I drive to the Krispy Kreme near my home and tell myself, "I'm just going in for ONE donut to feed my fix and then I'm outta there."

Darn if I didn't have to go there on a Sunday morning when the line was out the door. Now, I don't ever mind waiting because you get to see the donuts being made behind the big glass wall. And if that is not enough to keep you captivated and entertained, they send an employee out to the waiting line with FREE food samples to try while you wait. But they don't just give you a sample-sized bite—oh NO—they have to give you the whole donut! Yes, the entire hot, fabulous, glazed, amazing, melt-in-your-mouth donut.

Now how am I going to go up to the register and buy just one donut? I can't! They did it again and triggered my obligation factor. You may not know where your obligation factor is located on your body but, believe me, you have a trigger.

So what do I do? I buy two huge boxes of donuts and then I try to think of who I can deliver them to so that I don't eat them all in one sitting. After all, I'm still working my way through that huge tub of chocolate chip cookie dough I got at Costco.

We all love to get FREE stuff, and when we do, it triggers the obligation factor. Humans just naturally want to return the favor when receiving. Here is another example. A high-end men's retail shoe store that I know of repays their customers when they sign up on the mailing list. They understand the value a new prospect's contact information can offer them. Therefore, they repay them with a gift of shoe polish just for signing up.

This smart retailer doesn't stop to think about how much the FREE item costs them to give away, because they look at the value of receiving a new prospect's contact information. That's priceless! When a prospect gives you their contact information, they are allowing you to market to them in the future. They would not do this if they didn't already show interest in you and what you have to sell.

Give something away for FREE and it will come back to you many times over in increased business and customer loyalty.

I've been giving away valuable gifts to my customers and clients for years and it has always come back to reward me in return. But my *ultimate gifts of appreciation* began in January 2005 when my dear friend Patricia Drain and I both formed our own seminar company called Maximizing Success, Inc. Together we felt that the best way to reward our clients would be to invite them to attend an amazing Customer Appreciation Wealth Building Boot Camp featuring over a dozen world-class speakers, experts, and authors. We footed the bill for the entire production and invited our customers and our speakers' customers to attend for absolutely FREE. The value of this event was nearly $1,800 per person, and we invited them to this entire three-day event for FREE. Yes FREE!

Why would we put ourselves at such financial risk to put on a huge event like this and invite people to come for nothing? Because we put our trust in the fact that those who attended also would trust the amazing value this life-changing event had to offer them. They, in turn, would invest in additional events and speakers' products to continue their personal growth and professional growth. We changed lives and started a successful new business at the same time.

To learn more about how you can attend our life-changing Wealth Building Boot Camps and Universities featuring dozens of world-class experts, speakers, and authors, visit our Web site at http://www.maximizingsuccess.com.

7

FORM NEW HABITS THAT SKYROCKET SALES

"Bad habits are like a comfortable bed, easy to get into, but hard to get out of."
UNKNOWN

The core of motivation that empowers your mind to think and act differently also will allow you to develop habits that change old belief systems. In fact, 95 percent of what you think and do every day is habitual. We live mostly by habit. Therefore, it is hard to bring about significant change without changes in behavior first.

Barriers to changing habits seem to be everywhere. We may be able to force ourselves, with mature will and self-discipline, to do certain unpleasant things in order to get very desirable results, but it is almost impossible to force ourselves to do so consistently.

WE ARE ALL CREATURES OF HABIT

We are all creatures of habit, meaning that no matter how hard we try to break out of old, worn-out selling routines (that don't work) and get fired up about a new way of doing things, we always slip back into the old patterns, the old habits. Simply put, it's easier to just do what we've always done. So we wind up just doing more of it, which gets us nowhere!

Because we are creatures of habit, we need to practice acting in spite of fear, in spite of doubt, in spite of rejection, in spite of worry, in spite of uncertainty, in spite of inconvenience, in spite of discomfort. We even need to practice when we're not in the mood to act.

We all can be re-created when we take revolutionary steps to achieve goals that are important to us. By being more aware of your underlying resistance to change, you can become more effective in generating positive change and meaningful growth. Knowing why you want to change in the first place is critical to your success. Often, we don't change until the pain or loss of not changing is powerful enough to move us to action.

How will changing your sales habits affect your outcome?

DEVELOPING ELEMENTS FOR CHANGE

The first element of change is awareness. You can't change something unless you are first aware of it. To be aware is to be awakened to new ways of thinking and new perceptions. Once you relate to a new way of thinking, you will move away from avoiding habits and change. Highly successful salespeople develop the ability to easily change their habits.

The second element of change is understanding. When you understand how your way of thinking has brought you to where you are today, you gain personal insight and knowledge regarding why you react in certain ways. When you can grasp the knowledge for more effective ways of selling and begin to see proven results, you'll be more open to creating life-changing habits instead of avoiding them.

The third element of change is disassociation. Once you realize that your old ways of thinking and reacting have not been in your best interest, you can separate yourself from unproductive habits.

The fourth element of change is reconditioning. Effective reconditioning will allow you to sell more effectively and help you stop wasting time by feeling down when sales are lost.

Would you be open to change if you would never again allow rejection to wipe you out emotionally? The fear of rejection holds too many salespeople back from achieving more. To recondition yourself to utilize more effective habits, you must first identify personal behavior that may be holding you back from initiating more sales opportunities.

The habit of avoidance is one of the hardest of all habits to break.

MASTERING CHALLENGES WITH CHANGE

Learning something new and completely different liberates the mind. Facing a challenge, meeting it and mastering it, helps build confidence. Learning to overcome fears or taking part in new, challenging activities uses the intuitive part of our brains. This part of the brain is the same part that's vital for creatively solving problems. People who can solve problems creatively also can create life-changing results.

When we find that we do not like the results we are getting, we need to discover how we can change our thinking or our beliefs to move us past obstacles.

The person in my life who taught me to accept change was my grandmother, Bernadette. Her amazing lesson in accepting change is both courageous and inspiring.

When my grandmother was 85 years old, she was not the healthy, active person she once was. Her arthritis, high blood pressure, and pain left her dependent on a walker or cane to get around. Pain pills and lots of sleep helped her cope with life on a day-to-day basis. It became frustrating to her when the doctors told her that there was nothing they could do to help because there was no cure for arthritis. At that point in her life, she was feeling weak and depressed.

She decided to try another doctor for one last hope. This doctor suggested that she try water aerobics. "Oh, no!" were the first words out of her mouth. "I never go into the water. I'm deathly afraid of it." And with her great sense of humor, she added, "The closest that I ever came to water was a walk on the beach—and even that made me nervous."

Reluctantly, she decided to give it a try as her last hope to rid herself of pain and get back on her feet. As she sat on the steps of the pool that first day, she was shaky and afraid to get in. Her therapist coaxed her to walk across the pool with the help of her walker.

Each day it became a little easier, and she started to build her confidence and her stamina. As she improved, she no longer needed the help of the physical therapist, and soon joined a local health club. Her first water aerobics instructor was a fit 90-year-old man retired from the military. He inspired her to continue and get even better.

After less than a year, my grandmother was free of pain and lived a very active lifestyle without the use of a walker or a cane. In fact, her last few years of life were some of her happiest and most fulfilling.

My grandmother lived to be 93 years young. Just three short weeks before she passed away, she actually was teaching water aerobics at the retirement community where she lived.

Hopefully, my grandmother's courageous story will inspire and motivate you to accept more positive changes in your life too.

DEVELOPING A COMMITMENT TO CHANGE HABITS

Mark LeBlanc, author of *Growing Your Business* and founder of SmallBusinessSuccess.com, says, "Too often, people in sales err on the side of the Great Commitment. They get sick and tired of being sick and tired, or not achieving their goals. Then they make the great commitment that now things are going to be different. They pledge to themselves and others that this is the dividing line in the sand, and then quickly proceed to make more calls than ever before, or go to more networking meetings than ever before. Soon, when things don't happen fast enough, their discouragement and frustration get the best of them and they fall into the Great Commitment once again. Only it gets harder and harder to pick themselves up, and time marches on. Their level of belief wavers, and their pilot lights begin to dim.

"Successful sales professionals who are in it for the long haul understand the value of their vision and taking action steps in a consistent fashion."

Mark shared two action steps you can take to move toward success:

1. Simply craft the profile of your ideal month with as much clarity and definition as possible. True professionals build their ideal month around numbers and activities, and remember to include the personal side of their lives as well.
2. Focus on the RRR Principle, which stands for realistic, regular, and reach. What can you realistically do, on a regular basis, in order to reach your goal?

When you focus on those monthly benchmarks that are achievable in a busy month as well as in a slower month, then you build a foundation for success that is unstoppable.

DEVELOP PERSISTENT BEHAVIORS

Successful salespeople develop the habit of being persistent. They are doers. They take immediate action to get positive results. They also are prepared and consistent with their selling habits. They are so good at selling consistently that they appear to have all the luck.

Luck doesn't happen by chance. Luck is what happens when preparation and circumstance meet. Planning will allow you to know what preparation you need in order to create more luck for yourself too.

Persistence requires the powerful attitude of determination. Determination moves you forward with a sense of purpose, will power, and fortitude that will allow you to move away from the negative habits that are holding you back.

Persistence is the number one characteristic needed to achieve your current and long-term goals. More than any other attribute you can possess, persistence is the most powerful.

You have the ability to succeed in sales. There is only one real difference between salespeople who exceed their goals and those who struggle each month to barely reach their goals. That one difference is the commitment to overcome the problems and obstacles every salesperson encounters during his or her sales career.

Persistence enables you to stay focused on goals, overcome obstacles and problems, and create the success you desire.

The Seven Powerful Ways to Develop Persistent Behaviors

1. Think flexibly to solve problems. Skilled salespeople are good problem solvers. They think flexibly to produce a variety of ideas, responses, questions, and solutions to their challenges. Flexible thinkers come up with numerous different ideas. When considering what to do about a situation, they shift their approach and take a detour in a new direction.

When you are considering what to do about a situation, shift approaches or change direction in thinking just as you would turn in a car when you encounter a detour. Seek as many different ideas, directions, or alternatives as you have time to consider. Think of how your positive habits will benefit your customers. Consider situations differently, from your customer's point of view.

Make up different scenarios, situations, or problems in your mind and figure out a way to overcome them. Think of a number of different possibilities for solving a problem. Flexible thinking will help you solve more problems and allow you to be ready for any sales challenge before it appears.

2. Be curious. Skilled salespeople are always curious. Curiosity is the most important characteristic of all learners. Someone who stays stuck has a certainty about how they view challenges versus someone who overcomes challenges more effectively by inquiring.

Become more curious about your surroundings. Observe keenly and ask questions. Find out about the people and the situations associated with the problem you are solving. Give yourself time to wonder, to explore, and to puzzle over things for a while. Question the way you usually solve problems. Search for strategies that bring you new ideas, and become more open to exploring the unfamiliar. Exploring and acting on what is unfamiliar helps you to change habits quickly.

3. Develop fluent thinking. A salesperson who allows their way of thinking to flow usually comes up with the most ideas, responses, solutions, or questions.

Always think of more than one answer. How you see your alternatives determines how fluent you are with your thinking. You can develop fluent thinking by generating a flow of answers to your questions. Create numerous ideas about how to solve different sales challenges. Work fast and produce more than other salespeople around you.

4. Generate original ideas. Salespeople who have strength in original thinking usually dream up unique solutions. They produce clever ideas rather than common or obvious ones. They delight in thinking and designing unusual approaches, and they choose to figure things out on their own.

Generate original ideas. Invent and celebrate your uniqueness. Think your own thoughts and be your own person. Think of exceptional responses to your customers' questions. Think of a new approach rarely thought of by others. Build your strengths by seeking a fresh approach to a stereotyped answer.

Dare to be different! Create a new twist in the way you think and react. Change old habits that only make you follow the crowd. Refuse to conform and be like others. Rebel against doing things the way everyone else does them. The more you conform to be like everyone else, the less successful you will be. Find your own way, figure out your own solutions, and enjoy the unusual.

5. Be more elaborate in your way of thinking. Successful salespeople elaborate on their ideas and stretch to move away from ineffective habits. People who elaborate in their thinking may not be originators, but once they get hold of a new idea, they modify or expand it.

Stretch and expand your thinking to different ways of selling. Seek to embellish solutions by making them interesting and fun. If you could count the number of times a person senses something lacking and adds details to improve on it, you can determine how elaborate a person is.

Be more elaborate in your way of thinking by creating a deeper meaning to someone else's great idea. I call this the RD&T method—rip off, duplicate, and tweak. There are not as many original ideas as there are ways of elaborating on what already exists.

6. Trust in the power of your imagination. The imaginative salesperson can conceptualize the future as something other than the past and move forward with new habits. People with strong imaginations recognize the difference between fantasy and reality and use it to their advantage.

Without imagination, you sabotage yourself and repeat the same mistakes over and over. With the power of imagination, you can visualize goals you have not yet achieved. Put your imagination first to proceed with the faith or hope of achieving your goals. You can develop your imagination by trusting your intuitive feelings or predicting what someone else has said or done without knowing the answer. Wonder about and imagine things that have never happened. Envision achieving your dreams and goals.

7. Develop courage by taking risks. Being courageous means doing something in spite of your fears, just as my grandmother did when she overcame her life-long fear of water to improve her health. Courageous people act in spite of fear, and they tackle uncertain and uncomfortable situations.

Take risks with care and courage. Be willing to make guesses and act on your hunches. Of course, you must take risks cautiously, once witnessing the best and worst possible results. This is where your imagination comes in handy; it is a terrific way to take chances without being foolhardy. You will find courage inherent in persistence.

To develop your powers of courage and take new strides in sales, be willing to defend your ideas regardless of what others think, even if you know you may be wrong.

Set high goals of accomplishment without fear of going for them. Admit your mistakes and let go of what others think or disapprove of about you. Hold fast to your choices to succeed. Often the choice to move away from the crowd or not to go with the flow is a difficult one to make, and that is why it takes courage. Yet, when you choose to move in a different direction, it often can empower the confidence you have in your own abilities.

For example, last year I made the tough decision to move away from a group of experts in one of my niche industries. This group had developed a partnership of working together and sharing leads by marketing their expertise as a collective group. I did believe that by being involved in this niche group, it would expand my opportunities within the industry. But, also, I more strongly believed that working alongside people who were not like-minded regarding my sales beliefs would do me more harm than good.

When one of the people on the team voiced her disapproval of how I promoted my products and services from the platform, I knew that our beliefs about selling were much different. Therefore, I felt that I had two choices: either adjust my way of selling or move away from aligning myself with the team altogether.

My decision to move away from aligning myself with this group of experts may or may not have been the right decision, but I had to trust my gut and support my own beliefs.

Trusting in yourself, your expertise, and your beliefs will allow you to develop the courage that is needed to take more risks.

HABITS THAT HOLD YOU BACK FROM INITIATING SALES OPPORTUNITIES

We all have behaviors or habits that hold us back in one form or another. When salespeople form limited behaviors or habits, they sabotage their sales opportunities. The more limiting the behavior, the more it prevents success. On the other hand, the most successful salespeople in the world learn how to overcome the personal behavior and habits that have sabotaged their opportunities in the past.

George Dudley and Shannon Goodson, authors of *The Psychology of Sales Call Reluctance*, have spent more than 25 years studying and researching sales success from a scientific perspective. They discovered 12 different types of sales Call Reluctance®, which they define as a learned, nonconscious behavior that prevents salespeople from initiating sales opportunities. Together they created a personal assessment that identifies the way we unconsciously avoid promoting or selling. Their research studies discovered that feeling comfortable with self-promotion is directly related to sales success. Hundreds of thousands of salespeople have taken the assessment and dramatically increased their sales because of it.

Below are six forms of Call Reluctance, excerpted from Dudley and Goodson's book:

1. *Yielder.* In sales, Yielders have difficulty asserting themselves, particularly when it comes to prospecting. Afraid to incite conflict or risk losing approval, Yielders become pathetically polite for the fear of appearing pushy or intrusive. Yielder Call Reluctance often contains a hereditary component, so it is not easily eliminated. Nevertheless, the outlook is still very positive.

2. *Referral Aversion.* For most salespeople, asking for referrals is appropriate and easy. For a call reluctant minority, however, it is difficult and distressing.

3. *Over-Preparer.* Over-Prepared Call Reluctance occurs in sensitive salespeople who become anxiously concerned about being swept away by the intensity of their own feelings. In sales, they tend to spend too much time preparing what to say and how to say it, while spending too little time prospecting for people to give their presentations to.

4. *Telephobia.* Telephobia Call Reluctance is a highly selective impairment. It is found only in salespeople who become distressed when they try to use a telephone as a prospecting tool.

5. *Stage Fright.* Fear of speaking before a group is a form of call reluctance that occurs in salespeople who are overanxious about their appearance. Stage Fright Call Reluctance appears to be entirely learned. It may come from inexperience as a group speaker or from an early traumatic experience associated with making a group presentation.

6. *Role Rejection.* Role Rejection Call Reluctance occurs when a salesperson is intellectually willing but emotionally unable to accept a career in sales. Role Rejection is tricky to diagnose accurately because the afflicted salesperson may be unaware of the problem except for the nagging feeling that he or she should be considering a career change.

Although it is difficult to diagnose, once it has been accurately detected and measured, it is among the easiest and fastest forms of call reluctance to correct.

Five Steps to Help You Push Through Any Call Reluctance

Call Reluctance licensee Jeffrie Story offers these five steps to help you push through any sales call reluctance:

1. Be aware of where you're avoiding making contacts.
2. Set daily goals for making contacts you've been avoiding, and reward yourself when you meet your goals—even if it's a star on your calendar.
3. Relax, recall past accomplishments, and mentally visualize yourself easily making those contacts.
4. Tell yourself you *can* jump over the temporary fear and discomfort.
5. Focus on your goals, and why you're making the contacts!

Jeffrie Story helps organizations and individuals turn hidden sales potential into money, through proven, scientific tools. By combining scientific tools with an extensive sales background and a passion for transformation, Jeffrie helps create behaviors that are consistent, sufficient, and effective. Learn more at UnleashYourSalesDNA.com.

Find Out Where You Are Losing Out on Sales Opportunities

Discover exactly why sales opportunities are slipping away from you, and how your own subconscious habits are limiting your sales success by taking the online sales assessment yourself. Learn how and why you're hesitating to sell and market yourself more effectively, now, at SkyrocketingSalesBook.com.

HABITS SIZZLING SALESPEOPLE HAVE IN COMMON

Patricia Drain, author of *Sell the Sizzle* and president of PatriciaDrain.com, had the opportunity to interview 177 top sales producers from all backgrounds, both male and female. "Each of these individuals knew exactly what I meant when I talked about selling the sizzle. After interviewing them, I discovered that each individual followed certain daily habits that took them to the level of Top Producer in their profession."

Following are the seven habits that top sales producers have in common:

1. They develop a PLAN. Sizzling salespeople plan their days, weeks, and months. They set goals in place and work their plan to exceed those goals.

2. They create a clear FOCUS. Sizzling salespeople ALWAYS stay focused on their specialty and their plan. They stay focused by prioritizing each day.

3. They ask QUESTIONS. Sizzling salespeople understand and utilize the art of asking the right questions. They list the RIGHT questions to ask when sizzle selling.

4. They SHARPEN their skills. Sizzling salespeople understand the importance of sharpening their saws. They invest in the resources needed to ensure ongoing training.

5. They understand the power of NUMBERS. They understand that to increase their sales, they must increase their prospects, customer base, and sales volume.

6. They know how to stay in CONTROL. Sizzling salespeople stay in control of themselves to stay on track. They use this control to keep a personal balance in their lives.

7. They have a strong BELIEF SYSTEM. Sizzling salespeople believe they are worthy of the highest earnings, commissions, or salary, and that their time is extremely valuable.

PRIORITIZE YOUR TIME

Much of the time salespeople are not actually involved in the selling process. Instead, they are doing other things associated with their job, such as prospecting, making calls, or doing paperwork. If you want your sales to skyrocket, you must make the best use of your time and prioritize your daily tasks.

Stay on track and don't allow yourself to get easily distracted. Stop wasting hours talking with other salespeople on the team or making calls to dead-end prospects. Don't spend too much time preparing for a sale. There will never be the perfect time for anything, so jump in with both feet and get going.

It is estimated that for every 20 calls you make, you'll get an appointment and/or make a sale. Therefore, it is important to maximize the best use of your calling time. Try to not overwhelm your schedule with appointments so that you have more time to make the calls that will turn leads into more sales.

Don't work harder—work smarter! Quit saying: "I would do that if I had more time." If you are saying that, it probably is NOT because you don't have the time, but because you are simply not making the BEST USE of your time. Stop doing things that waste time and make you work harder. Begin to prioritize each day by doing only the things that get you more business.

After my presentations I always have audience members approach me to ask questions. Often they want my advice on how to overcome their biggest business obstacle. The question that is most frequently asked is, "How do I find the time to do all of the things you suggested that will help my business grow?" They then usually continue the conversation by telling me about 20 things they are doing and how it is hard to keep up.

It is easy for me to see that they are so overwhelmed that it is hard for them to think—much less be productive. It is apparent that their overwhelming feelings are holding them back from ever reaching their peak potential. When I see this to be true, I usually will take them aside of the crowd to talk with them one-on-one. I put my hands on their arms, look them right in the eye, and ask them to take a deep breath.

"Obviously you are working way too hard, so let me help you. It appears that you are a bit overwhelmed, so it is important that you first refocus your energies. When you take the time to do that, you will start to see the value of implementing the proven business strategies that I've shared with you. You will begin to move ahead instead of doing things that make you work harder and hold you back. You will instantly stop wasting your time and begin to use your talents in ways that will reap you the fastest return on your valuable time. Does that sound like something you would like to know more about?"

I suggest that they FOCUS on three things every day that put them in a position to exceed their goals. If you could only FOCUS on three things a day that would skyrocket your sales, what would they be?

List the three daily tasks that would give you the best return on your investment in time:

1. _____
2. _____
3. _____

Note that these are the things you should be doing every day. Prioritize your list so that you get those things completed every day. Either delegate the rest or let it go. You can't do it all, but you CAN learn how to work smarter when you focus on your three ROTI (return on time investment) tasks.

Did you know what the number one reason is that stops people from getting what they want? It's lack of FOCUS. People who focus on what they want, prosper. If you want to exceed your goals, you must develop the power of focus and visualization. The best book that I've ever read on this topic is *The Power of Focus* by Jack Canfield, Mark Victor Hansen, and Les Hewitt. This book made me stop and think about how I could best invest my time, and it helped me to learn how to work smarter from that day forward.

The bad news is that you can't create more time. Each hour has only 60 minutes, each day only has 24 hours, and each week only has 7 days. But the good news is that you can learn to focus on prioritizing your day. When you do, you will begin to work smarter by investing your time and talents in areas that give you the greatest return.

HOW DO YOUR SERVICE HABITS MEASURE UP?

Now that we have discussed sales habits, let's focus on the habits that you have already formed to service your customers well. To evaluate your own sales service habits, read the 40 questions below. As you read along, put a check mark in front of all the questions that you can easily and honestly answer with a YES. Note: Be completely honest with yourself—this is the only way you can form more productive service habits.

_____1. Do you avoid judging others when you first meet them and give everyone the same respect and courtesy?

_____2. Do you continually take the time to learn more about how to improve your sales skills with an open mind?

_____3. Are you well prepared before every sales call?

_____4. Do you prioritize your work with sales at the top of the list every day?

_____5. Do you make every effort to focus on a positive attitude and to radiate contagious enthusiasm every day?

_____6. Do you understand who your core customer is and what triggers them to buy?

_____7. Are you getting into the minds and hearts of a core target market with your sales and marketing message?

_____8. Do you know why a prospective customer would want to buy from you instead of your competitor?

_____9. Do you have a personal USP (unique selling position)?

_____10. Do you have sales goals written out for the next six months to three years?

_____11. Do you speak your goals out loud to others in the form of affirmations?

_____12. Do you visualize your sales success at the start of each day?

_____13. Do you listen well and ask questions that allow you to have a complete understanding of your customer's needs, wants, and/or concerns?

_____14. Are you always honest with your customers?

_____15. Do you avoid aggressive sales behavior at all times?

_____16. Do you respect your customer's right to reject and/or object to your offer?

_____17. Do you send business to your friendly competitors when you can't make a sale?

_____18. Are you focused on always making the customer feel important?

_____19. Do you return a customer's call promptly when they have a problem or concern?

_____20. Do you have an organized system for follow-up and follow-through?

_____21. Do you offer your customers a reward for their referrals?

_____22. Do you send personalized thank you notes to your customers for their business and referrals?

_____23. Do you seek out innovative ways to sell and market to prospective customers?

_____24. Do you stay in touch with existing customers through a direct mail piece a minimum of six times a year?

_____25. Do you diversify your sales message to different genders and generations?

_____26. Do you listen 70 percent or more of the time during your sales presentation?

_____27. Do you consider yourself a resource and/or support system for your customers?

_____28. Do you sincerely empathize with your customers' concerns and problems?

_____29. Do you enjoy solving problems and/or discovering innovative solutions to the needs of your customers?

_____30. Do you consider yourself a real "people person" who loves meeting new people?

_____31. Do you know the details about your products and/or services inside and out?

_____32. Do you get to know all that you can about the competition, including their strengths and weaknesses, inventory, and/or services?

_____33. Do you consider yourself a knowledgeable "expert" within your industry?

_____34. Do you have a sales mentor who keeps you motivated and inspired?

_____35. Do you go beyond your customers' expectations with added value?

_____36. Do you read sales books and trade journals within your industry to keep your knowledge and expertise cutting-edge?

_____37. Have you introduced yourself to complementary companies where your customers also buy from, and created alliances to share referrals?

_____38. Do you promote yourself effectively within your community on a regular basis?

_____39. Do you attend networking events to seek out prospective customers and new business alliances?

_____40. Are you ASKING your customers for testimonials and using them in your marketing message?

Next, rate yourself on the scale below by adding up all the Yes responses on your list.

0–20	You've got a lot to learn about selling effectively. Read, study, and learn from other successful salespeople. Be a sponge for knowledge!
15–25	Reevaluate your sales and service strategies. Ask for help and change ineffective habits!
25–35	Good job! You are a sales pro who is open to constant improvement and learning new habits. Keep learning, growing, and improving all the time.
35–40	You are working at your peak sales potential. Keep up the great work and mentor others who need your support.

"All roads lead to success—even the detours."
ANONYMOUS

8

MANAGE ANY CUSTOMER RESISTANCE

"Success is to be measured not so much by the position that one has reached in life as by the obstacles which have been overcome while trying to succeed."
BOOKER T. WASHINGTON

Where does a high level of confrontational resistance come from? The strongest, healthiest self-confidence that you can build!

In the past, traditional sales taught you to overcome objections. But with today's customer, you simply need to manage objections. Consider any objection, resistance, or complaint as a way to get better. When a customer offers resistance, indirectly, he or she is trying to guide you on how to improve.

It is necessary to monitor your prospect's feedback and continually adjust your course of action. When a customer resists, it is simply a nudge for you to move in another direction. You are being told to take another road or see it from another view—your prospect's point of view. With nonverbal communication, your prospect is saying, "Don't go down that road. Let's go my way instead."

Resistance should be viewed as an opportunity, not a roadblock. The prospect is letting you get to know him or her better, and helping you to uncover his or her needs, wants, and concerns more effectively. A prospect who shows resistance to something is actually participating in the sale and connecting with you at some level, instead of moving away from it. When handled correctly, this opportunity can be turned into a positive, long-lasting customer relationship.

Resistance can take on many forms, such as questions, statements, and body language, and can mean many things. Occasionally, it is difficult to understand the exact reason for the resistance because people use excuses to cover up their true feelings. Prospects don't like to say NO. Your prospects or customers are actually doing you a favor if they are honest and straightforward when they tell you how you let them down. This is helpful feedback that will allow you to improve for the next opportunity.

If the reason for the resistance is incorrect or insufficient information, determine where you may have gone wrong and why. Did you give incorrect or incomplete information? Did you give too much information that left the prospect confused? Did your prospect resist due to not understanding or a breakdown in communication? Did your prospect resist because you added pressure to the sale?

Whatever the situation, go back and reevaluate your prospect's resistance to buying. Learn from the resistance by gathering more information, following up with correct information, reevaluating your selling strategies, and/or improving your own communication skills. Really listen and carefully observe both verbal and nonverbal communication with your prospect. Clarify the basis of the prospect's resistance so that you'll travel down the right road next time around.

REJECTION COMES WITH THE TERRITORY

I'm not going to tell you that you'll never get rejected; and I'm not going to say that there won't be days when, despite all your best efforts, you feel like you're simply not getting anything accomplished. Some days you may feel that every call you make, and every appointment you go on, is part of a spiraling sales cycle of rejection.

Selling isn't always smooth sailing, and if you see enough prospects, you're bound to run into your share of objections. But if you took away the objections, salespeople would be reduced to nothing more than glorified order takers.

> *"When it is dark enough, you can see the stars."*
> **RALPH WALDO EMERSON**

Nobody likes rejection, and it's natural to feel some disappointment when you hear someone say NO. Yet the only surefire way to avoid rejection is to never ask for anything. And if you avoid rejection altogether, that is just what you will get—nothing.

Nevertheless, you must find an internal reservoir of strength, confidence, and security in your identity as a professional, and you must convey all of that to your prospect as an equal. Because that's what you are—a sales professional!

The best salespeople are never pushy and don't resort to hard-selling strategies. They understand that to be effective, they must allow the sale to take its own course and move at its own pace.

Great salespeople want their prospects to BUY, not to be rushed, pushed, or SOLD. They also understand that their prospects may have doubts, fears, and temptations that may cause them to avoid confrontation the majority of the time. Great salespeople understand this and quickly welcome questions and objections from their prospects with confidence, knowing that they have the ability to solve any problems or concerns. It is your job as a salesperson to be open to rejection and to solve problems.

Teach yourself to accept the fact that the prospect saying NO is not a reflection on you personally. So don't be too hard on yourself. Most prospects are merely saying NO for their own personal reasons or they simply don't want to make a decision at all. The best salespeople know that their prospect wants them to be convinced, sincere, and reassuring, and to help the prospect act rather than to avoid or postpone a decision.

The main obstacle in approaching the issue of rejection is not how the prospect thinks of you, but how you think of yourself. It can be difficult to bounce back from refusal and frustration, but you can when you have complete sales confidence. Learn to move away from rejection and on to the next sales opportunity. Your self-confidence will be strengthened by the next sales victory.

When rejection happens, gently question your prospect, keeping in mind that his or her resistance may be caused by one or more of the following reasons. For example, the prospect

- doesn't have a need for your product or service,
- lacks the funds or budget to buy your product or service,
- lacks the ability to buy due to lack of authority,
- lacks enough information to make an intelligent decision,
- lacks trust in you and/or trust in your company,
- was not interested in the first place and had no intention of buying,
- has a buying style that does not match your selling style,
- simply doesn't like you or has a personality conflict (it happens),
- has no urgency to buy, therefore, they have time to think it over,
- is not motivated to buy and just checking in for future reference,
- is pressured by lack of time and/or personal stress, and/ or
- did not get any needs, concerns, or buying questions resolved by the salesperson.

BECOME SOLUTION-ORIENTED

Successful salespeople are solution-oriented; that is, they spend their time and energy strategizing and planning the answers to challenges that come their way. They see problems as challenges and obstacles to overcome. Once overcoming the obstacle, they put systems in place to avoid the same problem in the future.

Are you solution-oriented or problem-oriented?

If you are problem-oriented, you probably spend too much time and energy complaining and whining about a situation instead of taking action to solve the challenge. Mistakes are simply challenges in disguise. We all make mistakes, but it is how you overcome the challenge that is most important. Those who know how to best overcome the challenges of resistance create more sales opportunities.

Do you make mistakes? Hopefully you answered YES, because that shows you are taking some risks that will move you toward success. Without risk, there is no reward. Yet with risk, there will be some challenges and obstacles in your way. Don't worry too much about those challenges and obstacles. When handled wisely, they will become your lessons in disguise.

You won't always do the right thing, and you will make some mistakes along your journey to success. There always will be customer challenges or buying obstacles that stop you in your path toward exceeding your goals—that's how business works. The good news is, though, that once you make these mistakes, you won't have to make them again. Taking calculated risks is like failing forward fast. Allowing yourself to be open to risk will help you to get those failures out of the way. Every successful salesperson has failed time and time again as they learned to become true professionals. Yet the difference between successful salespeople and those who are not is that successful salespeople open themselves up to more risk, they don't allow failure to stop them, and they keep discovering the solutions to their sales challenges.

Every salesperson at every level of success has lessons to learn. Often, the only way to learn them is through the failures and mistakes that occur along the way. You're not going to make every sale, and not everyone is going to like you! Period! Some customers you can't win over or win back no matter how hard you try. There are always those few customers that no one can please. Some people are just difficult, argumentative, uncooperative, nasty, cantankerous, cynical, and sour on life! These prospects are not worth your time.

What do you do when you have to deal with people like this? The temptation is to spout off and turn your energy into a negative force to combat theirs. But don't go there! You don't have to defend yourself, and you don't have to worry about what their problem is. What people say to you cannot annoy or irritate you unless you give it permission to do so. The only way other people can upset you is if you allow them to do so. Do not permit prospects to detour you from your joy of selling, your confidence, and your strong self-image. Don't allow them to drag you down, because if you do, they'll try to make their problems yours. You can believe the old saying that "misery loves company."

Negative, downer people are one of my biggest pet peeves. During my many years in sales, I had to fire a few bad customers, asking them to go away forever and never return. It's amazing how much life one negative person can suck out of an entire team of salespeople. I couldn't afford to allow one really bad customer to affect my entire sales team when they had to be UP for all the good customers who came in after them.

With so much opportunity and joy in the world, I can't understand why people choose to be negative. And that's not your choice either. It's theirs. You choose to be happy, positive, and up. So take their resistance in stride and move away as fast

as you can. Send these negative downers to your competition—
the competitors you don't like.

DON'T LET FRUSTRATION LEAD TO RESENTMENT

Frustration over handling sales resistance will stifle most salespeople's level of success. Occasionally, this type of frustration can lead to resentment. Have you ever resented the idea that some customers or prospects have had control over your sales success?

If you respond to your lack of sales by blaming outside influences out of frustration, you are killing your self-confidence. When you make comments such as "That stupid customer can't make up their mind," "The economy is awful," "No one is coming in because of the lousy weather," "The competition is cutting prices so low that we can't compete," and the like, you give up all your power and accept helplessness. There is no point in paying attention to creating more sales when you give up your power to be successful. When you give up, you also allow your self-confidence to shrink dramatically.

When you blame, you give up power. When you accept responsibility for your own sales frustrations, you gain power.

Focus on cooperation and you will automatically eliminate customer conflict.

Most salespeople see objections as frustration too. They view objections as resistance, and when it occurs, resent it. But when you look at selling as servicing, you avoid conflict. Why? Because conflict and cooperation cannot exist in the same place at the same time!

"True genius resides in the capacity for evaluation of uncertain, hazardous, and conflicting information."
WINSTON CHURCHILL

Turn your frustration into humor when you can. It's hard for me to imagine anyone who doesn't have a sense of humor, although I have met a few people that I wondered about. So, assuming that you have a sense of humor, putting some fun and lightheartedness into your sales presentation can be an appropriate way to break the ice when times get tense. Injecting humor at the right time can be an excellent way to get back to solid ground by allowing your customer to find a way to relax and maybe even smile.

Remember, we're talking sales here—not brain surgery! Relax and have some fun when trying to win over a bad situation.

HANDLE ANY OBJECTION WITH CONFIDENCE

Sales professionals deal with objections in almost every sale. The reason some objections occur in the first place is because of poor sales presentations, so to reduce the risk of objections be sure to give a thorough sales presentation. The more complete the presentation, the more clearly the buyer will understand your offer, which, in turn, will provide them with more reasons to make a positive buying decision.

One objection that frustrates most salespeople is, "I want to think it over." In this case, the prospect simply doesn't want to make a buying decision, and it's not necessarily because they object to you or what you have to sell. By telling you what they won't buy, the customer is also leading you in the direction of what they would buy if circumstances were right.

Objections also occur as a result of unconvincing sales presentations. A truly convincing presentation can melt away all remaining resistance. Deliver a convincing sales presentation by first boosting your confidence and developing a strong self-image. Secure your position by developing unshakable confidence in your products and/or services, and showcase them with enthusiasm.

Another way to reduce objections is to realize that some objections are raised with enough regularity to become predictable. Be ready for them before they occur. Simply by thinking through some of the objections your prospects may voice, you set yourself up to respond with awareness and confidence.

Realize that your answer to every objection doesn't have to be 100 percent satisfactory. With this in mind, if your prospect doesn't like every feature of your product, don't assume you've lost the sale. Your competition won't have a perfect product either.

Objections are simply expressions of interest.

Ignoring objections, problems, and/or concerns won't make them go away. The good news is that customers don't expect you to be perfect all of the time. They do, however, expect you to be honest with them all of the time. If you simply ignore problems or concerns instead of putting them out on the table and dealing with them, you will lose your customer's trust.

Take action quickly. Don't be afraid to return a customer's call when you know they have a problem. In fact, return the call promptly! If you don't, you could be turning a small problem into a much larger one. Once that happens, the customer may never do business with you again. Worse yet, they may tell more customers about the bad experience they had with you, and you don't ever want that to happen to you. Your professional sales reputation is at stake here.

I welcome objections that specifically state what the prospect doesn't like about my product or service. It allows me to focus on what it would take to get them to buy, and it teaches me a lot about selling effectively to the next prospect.

Don't dwell on an objection. Once you believe that an objection has been satisfactorily answered, move on quickly. Don't reply with "Well, what do you think now?" or "Does that settle your problem?" You don't need confirmation; just assume it.

Let prospects provide the needed objection so that they can form a logical conclusion around their emotions or attachment to what you are selling. Repeat their comments and thank them for their observations. Allow them to understand that there is no pressure to buy, and allow customers to take control over the buying decision. Make them feel good about voicing their opinions or objections. Some customers just want to be heard, and once you show that you are a good listener and support their interest, you instantly begin to gain trust. When you gain their trust, you begin to remove objection barriers that hold the customer back from buying.

Customers often put off until tomorrow only those decisions they lack the confidence to make today. Assuming that you have presented all of the facts necessary for the customer to make a buying decision, one reason for procrastination may remain: The customer is afraid of making the wrong decision. In this case, the customer would rather do nothing.

Your prospects will catch your enthusiasm and mimic your excitement as easily as they will mimic your lack of enthusiasm or hesitation. Pay attention to what your sales presentation is telling your prospects. I've seen more salespeople blow opportunities because they lacked sales confidence when it came down to overcoming an objection.

Begin by enthusiastically informing your prospects about how they can benefit from your product or service, and how it represents an excellent value for their time and money.

Help your customers make the RIGHT buying decisions. Take your time. There is no need to rush. Practice patience and stay focused on your customers' needs, wants, and concerns.

Don't ever rush the sale, sell for the sole purpose of your own gain, or insult a prospect's opinions. By judging a prospect's opinion because it differs from your own, you will be making the mistake of putting down your prospect.

I recently felt this type of put down when selecting flooring, cabinets, and lighting for the new house I was building. I've done a lot of moving, buying, and selecting by trusting my own opinions for years. In fact, I've built and sold nine new homes in the course of the past 18 years. And that only accounts for a small percentage of the houses I've invested in and improved on through my real estate investment company. By now I should know a thing or two about selecting interior design items, so when a salesperson puts down my opinions, I don't respond well.

The salesperson who was helping me select items for my home actually told me that my opinions were wrong. When you tell your customers they are wrong, you alienate any opportunity to connect with them.

"What you selected is not the right choice for your home. I think it is a mistake and wouldn't put that in my home," she said.

This salesperson had no intention of listening to and/or supporting my needs or concerns. She was not concerned with my opinions and, in fact, my objections only made her work harder at trying to prove me wrong.

She made it obvious to me that her only interests were to create an up-sell for her own higher sales commission, to rush me through the sale to control any additional objections, and to put down my choices so that I would move to her way of thinking. Needless to say, the sale went downhill from there.

If you view your prospect as an adversary, someone you are going to outsmart or show up, you are never going to be successful. Instead, you will lose that potential customer, and probably build a bad reputation in the process.

No, Not Interested!

Dottie Walters, author of *Never Underestimate the Selling Power of a Woman,* says, "Each sale is as exciting, different, and individual as the person who is purchasing. It can be an easy sale or a hard one—depending on your prospect and on your sales ability. The reason some sales come hard is because you meet resistance from the customer either in objections, excuses, or just plain 'NO, not interested.'"

Following are Dottie's five techniques that will help you turn a hard NO into an easy YES:

1. *Don't confuse the buyer's decision with too many choices.* Try to present not more than three choices to your buyer, tailored to fit their needs. Should the customer be wavering, your confidence and assumption will convince them that they made the correct choice.

2. *Find out the reason behind their NO.* Establish a "me too—I understand" feeling with your customer, and he or she will eventually tell you in word or action the reason behind the NO. Once you have this, you can easily bring up sales points that overcome it. Learn what your customer's problems are, talk about them, and try to make sincere suggestions. Then show the customer how the benefits of your product or service will solve his or her problems.

3. *Know when to leave your prospect alone.* Respect your customers' right of privacy and comply with their request. Your business is to show customers you have what they need. Their decision to buy or not to buy will be their own free choice. Customers can only respect you when you first respect them.

4. *Give yourself away, you'll never "Run Out!"* Give of yourself—your interest, your compassion, your sympathy, and your creative thoughts. Give continually over and beyond the call of duty and it will come back to you a thousandfold.

5. *Keep your prospect in the conversational picture.* Get to know your customers first. If you jump in too fast or run through your sales talk breathlessly, you will leave them cold. Why? Because you have excluded them from the conversation! Customers want to be part of it.

GET WHAT YOU DESERVE

Nido Qubein, author of *How to Be a Great Sales Professional*, says, "Life does not give you what you want or need—it gives you what you deserve. So to get more of what you deserve, offer more value. Your value as a salesperson is measured by the size of customer problems we're capable of solving. To increase our value, we must learn/observe more and develop relational capital with qualified prospects/customers.

"Treat every customer as if you're about to lose them and recognize that trust is the foundation for building success and significance in a client relationship. An extraordinary sales professional can sell a mediocre product faster and more profitably than can a mediocre salesperson sell an excellent product. We become excellent by growing and evolving our competence thru knowledge, skills, and experience."

> *"Competence leads to confidence and confidence leads to commitment."*
> **NIDO QUBEIN**

When you offer value to your prospects, you offer them the worth, importance, and usefulness of what you have to sell. Assess the value of what you have to offer your prospects.

Even when you offer value there sometimes will be sales challenges that you will need to overcome. Be prepared to handle your customer's value challenges quickly. When communicated properly, words of value can be like music to your prospect's ears.

Follow-up and follow-through is essential when trying to establish yourself as someone who adds increased value to your prospects' lives. More times than not, customers have made purchases solely because the sales professional communicated great value to them. Sales professionals know how to persuade prospects to buy their products or services based on the increased value they offer to their lives. What values do you offer your prospects that they can't refuse?

> *"People don't care how much you know*
> *until they know how much you care."*
> **UNKNOWN**

BUILDING SUCCESSFUL RELATIONSHIPS

9

LET YOUR FANS DO THE TALKING

"Internalize the Golden Rule of sales that says: 'All things being equal, people will do business with, and refer business to, those people they know, like, and trust.'"
BOB BURG

Referrals are the support system of any sales business. Every salesperson with an endless stream of referrals has instant peace of mind.

Are you getting enough referrals? If not, why aren't you getting them? Wouldn't it be great if all of your customers came from referrals? Wouldn't that make your job easier?

You are probably doing everything you can to provide excellent products and deliver the highest quality of service. No doubt you have a great reputation and your customers already love you. If that's really the case (and I believe it is), why aren't you getting all the referrals you deserve?

Would you like to know how to turn every customer into a steady stream of referrals? Wouldn't that make your job easier? The good news is that your existing customers who are pleased with their purchases and your service will automatically want to help you out with more referrals.

These verbal compliments easily can be turned into written testimonials or third-party endorsements that the salesperson can use to win over more prospective customers. Learn the art of asking for more referrals and testimonials, and reap the benefits by winning over more prospective customers.

Studies have proven that the one reason why salespeople don't get more referrals is simply because they don't ASK. There are two reasons why this happens: they either forget, or they don't have a strong enough relationship with their customers, so they don't feel comfortable enough to ASK.

The truth is that every sales professional should strive to have as much of his or her business as possible come from referrals. Why? Because referrals provide much more value than any other type of marketing you can create. The benefits of referrals are unquestionable, and the value of word-of-mouth advertising is priceless!

Here are some of the reasons why referrals offer such priceless opportunities:

- Referrals open doors of opportunity that you cannot open on your own.
- Referrals give you more credibility and pre-sell your expertise.
- Referrals make your job easier and more enjoyable.
- Referrals are more motivated to do business with you.
- Referrals are more profitable than chasing after prospects who don't know you.

So how do you get more referrals? First, get comfortable with asking. The worst your customers can say is no. But most likely, they will say YES. Most salespeople who already ask for referrals don't do it on a consistent basis, so it is important to systemize the way you ask for them. You must ask on a consistent basis.

Do not be too general and ask, "Who else do you know?" This will have them thinking about too many people, and they'll end up saying, "I can't think of anyone. I'll call with some names later." We all know what happens "later." You never get the call or the e-mail.

Plant referral triggers throughout the sales process. During a conversation, ask your customers to mention others who can utilize what you have to offer instead of waiting for them to get back with you. Don't count on them remembering your name or the name of your company. Pass out lots of business cards. They are inexpensive and powerful marketing tools.

Another good time to ask for referrals is when your customer is raving about you, your company, and your product and/or your services. What do you say when a customer gives you a compliment? Do you simply say "Thank you" and stop at that, or do you see this as a golden opportunity to ask for referrals? After you receive the compliment, continue your conversation with, "Thank you very much. A wonderful testimonial like that would really help my business and also would help a lot of other people have the same wonderful buying experience that you did. May I ask you to refer my services to your friends, family, and business associates?" Your customer most likely will reply with an agreeable YES.

Next, tell them how and when they should refer you. Tell them exactly what you would like them to do when they refer you. Don't leave it up to chance, and don't leave out the details. For example, if you are selling something for their new home or yard, ask your customers to take some of your business cards and keep them handy in a kitchen drawer to pass out when they receive compliments from visitors. When company comes to visit, we all have a tendency to hang out in the kitchen because it's relaxed and comfortable. Now that you've planted the seed in your customers' minds by telling them exactly how to refer you, they will remember and have instant access to your card.

I had a chiropractor who was great about asking for referrals. Because he had eliminated my pain and got me feeling better, he asked if I would refer him when others told me of their pain too. He said, "You can help out other people you know that may be in pain too by passing out my cards. Keep them in your wallet, and when you are talking with someone who can use my help, please give them my card."

REFERRAL REWARDS ARE A POWERFUL MARKETING TOOL

To kick your referral business into high gear, offer a referral reward. Find a way to reward your customers for every referral they send you. Make sure that you systemize this process so that you can test the effectiveness of your referral rewards. Be consistent so you never forget to pass along the reward that you promised your customer. The more consistent and systemized you are about asking for referrals and offering rewards, the more effective your results will be.

The first time I purchased a swimming pool for a new home I was building, I contacted and made appointments with six different pool companies. Because it was a large purchase for me, I was fearful that I would either make a mistake or get taken for a ride. I knew that I had to do my research first. What helped me make my final decision was, first and foremost, the relationship and trust I had built with the salesperson.

Every salesperson and pool company had a completely different style of selling. Each created an entirely different buying situation. One salesperson was not responsive and took too much time to return my call. I figured that if they took that long to get back with me when they wanted business, imagine how long it would take them if I had a problem. Another large organization made me feel like a NUMBER instead of a person. I didn't feel comfortable going with a company that didn't make a personal connection. I felt that if I had a concern, I would be moved from person to person, or possibly get stuck in voice mail when I tried to call with a question. Another used ineffective, pushy traditional selling strategies that turned me off. He did come in with the lowest bid though, so I kept him in the loop.

Then I met Dave from Safari Pools. He came to me by a referral from a good friend. I instantly had more trust in working with Dave, before I met with him, because of this great referral. Dave began the sales presentation by building an even more trusting relationship. He then shared his expertise and portfolio, and told me what he would be offering with his services and follow-up. He said, "I'm probably going to bug you with all of my follow-up. I plan on following up with you every step of the way as your pool is being built. I want you to be completely happy with the results, and also want to address any concerns or questions you may have along the way. I understand this is a big investment for you, and I'm sure you are concerned about doing it right and don't want to have any problems. I can assure you that my team is very skilled and professional."

He continued his presentation by telling me that he would start the pool the day after I closed on my new home. I thought, oh sure, like he is really going to do that; but I also felt that if he put it out there, he would be starting soon after I moved in.

Then the clincher of the sale came when Dave told me that not only would he beat anyone's price, he would offer a referral reward of $500 for every person I referred him to that purchased a pool or spa. Now that got me to pay attention!

Dave's bid came in higher than the "pushy" salesperson's quote, so I called him to tell him about it and to see if he could match it. He asked me to fax it over to him, and when he called me back, he pointed out how the "pushy" guy had left out a number of things that were necessary to complete my pool correctly. I was already looking for a way to do business with Dave because I trusted his referral, so when he went over every detail, making it easy for me to understand why his price was higher, it made me feel comfortable with my decision to do business with him. Oh yeah, and then there was that $500 bonus every time I referred him. Why do you think my friend referred him to me in the first place?

Dave did everything he promised he would do in the sales presentation and then some. He designed my entire landscaping even though he was not a landscaper, and he showed up to start my pool the afternoon of the day I closed on my new home.

I'm not usually a neighborly person, because I spend a lot of time out of town, but his huge referral reward got me to be neighborly—quickly. I was knocking on my neighbors' doors introducing myself, and then asking if they planned on putting in a pool. If they said yes, I invited them over to see my beautiful yard and then handed them one of Dave's business cards out of my kitchen drawer.

Although Dave did everything right with his presentation, follow-up, service, and referral reward, he did one thing wrong. He referred me to a landscape company that he basically just handed the business to. Wouldn't you love to have a business alliance that does the work for you (in this case drawing out landscape plans) and then hands that customer to you like a gift? Sure, we all would! Well they took the gift, did their job, and then went away without even a thank-you.

I believe that when someone hands you business, you need to do everything you can to keep not only that business happy, but the referral customer as well. You see, I think that any company that does business with you should be staying in contact with you after the sale. Not only to follow up and thank you, but to stay in the loop to get more business and/or more referrals. This landscape company never called to see if I was satisfied, never sent me a thank-you note, never asked for referrals, and never marketed to me to see if I could use their services again down the road.

I wasn't worried about having a problem with Dave's company, but I did end up having a concern with the landscape company. They didn't follow-up to handle the problem, but Dave did, and he became my ally to resolve the issue. Shortly after that he was looking for a new landscape company to refer business to.

I heard from that landscape company again about three years after I had moved into the house. They called and asked me to call them back to set up an appointment for them to stop by and take pictures of my yard for their portfolio. What? Were they crazy? They wanted me to call them back after no contact whatsoever, and help them to promote their business with no reward or benefit to me. I don't think so!

REFERRAL BUSINESS CREATES WARM LEADS

Referral business is generally much more rewarding than cold calling. Increasing your referral business will make your job easier, your work more profitable, and your life more enjoyable.

Prospecting is, and always will be, a key to building a business based on referrals, word-of-mouth advertising, and testimonials. However, despite its importance, it's surprising how many people still use ineffective traditional sales techniques.

As noted earlier, today's customers are more knowledgeable, less trusting, and want to have a "know you, like you, trust you" relationship with their salesperson. Once trust and truth are developed in this "new" customer's mind, the walls come down and you can begin to build an effective buyer/seller relationship.

Be up front with your customers, otherwise, those promises will kill your chances of generating repeat business and referrals. Keep in mind that customers will do business with, and refer business to, those people they know, like, and trust. Customers must feel this way to refer you. In other words, if they don't feel like they know, like, and trust you, then nothing you do will bring forth a referral. Still, that alone is not enough. You must create a referral system that works effectively for your customers, and one that makes it easy for them to relate to. Referrals are the result of doing the correct things in the referral-gathering process.

NETWORKING DYNAMICS

One smart salesperson can do a lot to increase sales for the organization. But put that salesperson's skills together with other great selling minds—sharing ideas and leads and brainstorming—then you have networking dynamics!

Brainstorming and networking with other like-minded salespeople are powerful tools to create more sales success. You can't just go it alone in this competitive marketplace. You need the help and knowledge of other successful people to stay on top of your game too.

Networking is not an option to becoming successful. It is a necessity! How can you possibly keep up to date and compete with the stiff competition without having that edge of additional knowledge and shared information? You can't!

Wouldn't you like to know how other salespeople motivate their teams, increase sales month to month, keep their customers satisfied, and so on? Wouldn't you like to know how they handle their day-to-day problems and challenges? Sure you would, and all you have to do is to network, get to know them, and share.

There is so much to learn, and we cannot do it all by ourselves. We need to share and network all of the time. There are opportunities out there just waiting for you, and all you have to do is to start looking for them. Every time you attend a tradeshow, convention, business function, chamber meeting, or seminar, networking opportunities await you.

You can start by meeting other salespeople at conventions during breaks and lunch. Talk to everyone, everywhere you go about your business. Don't be shy—introduce yourself and start sharing. When you take the time to share, so will they. Exchange business cards and keep in touch with your new sales associates. When you speak with other salespeople who are not direct competitors, you can share and learn everything about each other's businesses.

By connecting with salespeople in complementary companies, you will gain an invaluable stream of qualified referrals and new prospective customers. For example, when I owned my retail women's apparel stores, I aligned myself with complementary companies that I met while networking. My best alliances were always other businesses that my type of prospect would do business with, such as beauty salons, spas, and other retail stores.

When I discovered these strong alliances, I made it a point to make a memorable impression on them. Instead of going up to them and telling them all about me and what I sold, I instantly showed my support to help them. For example, I would say, "I would like to help you be more successful!" That always got their attention fast. I would add, "It appears that we have the same type of customer." Then I would ask them to describe their best customers to me. "That sounds just like the type of customers I do business with. We should get together and discuss how we can be referring one another more business. I would like to learn more about your organization and what you have to offer, and possibly send some warm leads your way. Would you be interested in getting together?" Yes is typically the answer. I'd conclude with, "I'll give you a call next week to set up a meeting. How about if I come by your business to see your operation, and then we can go to lunch from there?"

Be open and make it easy for them to say yes. When developed, this networking skill alone will skyrocket you right past any of your competitors.

Meet with your alliances on a regular basis. Discuss how you can share leads and referrals and send them business. What you put out there will come back to you many times over—so keep sending them referrals and new business. You'll be amazed just how quickly your business will grow through networking and sharing.

Commit to making networking a part of your ongoing marketing plan. Think of networking as a necessity to discover additional contacts and referrals. I'm sure you're working in your own business or organization every day, and you probably find it hard to get the time to network. But when you GET OUT and work ON your business instead of just IN it, you'll quickly uncover the rewards that networking has to offer. For example, networking offers some of these great benefits:

- You can develop strong business alliances that can promote you back.
- You can meet new people and develop new friendships who will send you referrals.
- You can share new ideas and sales strategies.
- You can discuss customer challenges and how to overcome them.
- You can inexpensively get warm leads of quality prospects.
- You can avoid having to make cold calls and chase down dead-end leads.

The following will help you to be effective when networking:

- Focus on getting to know the other person first.
- Share your message with confidence and enthusiasm.
- Work on remembering names using good listening skills and taking notes.

- Make good eye contact. The eyes are the most descriptive of all body parts. Others can tell by your eyes if you are sincere, honest, and interested in them.
- Send a handwritten greeting card to each new associate you meet within 24 hours.
- Always have business cards on hand for networking opportunities.

TESTIMONIALS MAGNIFY YOUR MARKETING EFFORTS

Prospects may not always believe what you have to say about your products or services, nor will they believe what your marketing has to say. But they will believe what your happy customers have to say about you and your organization. That is why using testimonials in all of your marketing and advertising will magnify your success rate.

So how do you get testimonials? Again, you ask. One of the best times to ask is when you receive compliments from a customers as mentioned earlier. Most of the time they will agree to write the testimonial for you when asked; however, don't sit around waiting for the testimonial letter to arrive in the mail because it probably won't. It's not that your customers are not being true to their word, but that they often lack the time or commitment to get it done.

Not only are people busy, but they also don't know what to say when writing the letter, so they avoid writing it altogether. To get around this, help them out and make it easy for them to give you the testimonial.

Here are three ways of going about it:

1. Write the testimonial yourself, based on some of the comments the customer shared with you. I often send my clients the testimonial via e-mail and ask them to

adjust it or add to it when they put it on their letterhead. You've got to be a bit gutsy, or as I would call it, "shameless," about writing your own testimonials if you want to get them back. I will then ask clients if they would like to scan the letter and send it to me via e-mail right away or put it in the mail. I prefer that they scan the letter for two reasons: first, so that I can get them to take action sooner, and second, so I don't have to worry if it gets lost in the mail. When you have a copy of the scanned testimonial, it is easy to save it to a file and forward on to clients when sending an online proposal.

2. Ask your customers to answer a few questions to get them thinking of why they would recommend you to others. Questions they can define, such as: "Why did you buy from me?" "How did our organization compare to our competitors?" "What type of experience did you have with your investment or purchase that would make you want to come back?"

3. Add a section to your letter of agreement that requests you receive a written testimonial once you've completed quality work. For example, this is what I add to every speaking agreement that goes out of my office: "A representative from XYZ organization will supply a reference letter on company letterhead after Debbie Allen has presented a dynamic program for your organization." Not only does this show my clients that I am 100 percent confident that my presentation will be dynamic and successful, it also reaps me tons of amazing testimonial letters from many different niche industries. You can never have too many testimonial letters. Having testimonials from different types of clients or organizations are helpful to show the diversity of your client range and also will expand your expertise.

Testimonials are evidence of goodwill, and should be treated as an asset to you and your company. They should be photocopied and used in proposal documents to create a portfolio for your office lobby, to showcase to prospective clients while on a sales call, and to use on your Web site, in your direct mail, and in your advertising.

Don't hesitate to do whatever it takes to satisfy your customers. You will be rewarded many times over with repeat business, referrals, and powerful testimonials—priceless and powerful marketing tools that will skyrocket your sales!

Don't Just Satisfy–Thrill Them! by Joel Weldon, Sales Trainer and Idea Consultant

"Debbie Allen already has told you how your customers must be pleased not only with what they invested in, but in you as well. Let's expand on that. What if you didn't just 'satisfy' your customers . . . you thrilled them! What if you absolutely blew their minds with such exceptional service and follow-through! Suppose you told your customer you'd do seven specific things after the sale and you did all seven. They would most likely be pleased. What if, instead of promising to do seven things, you committed to do three and then you actually did seven. They would be thrilled!

"The key to thrilled customers who will be willing to give you referrals and sing your praises is best expressed in six words, 'Promise A Lot, Deliver Even More.' That's it. It's not just under-commit and over-deliver. It's promise a lot more than your competitors do and then deliver even more! One of those 'even more' actions is going back for an in-person service call, actually showing your customers something new that they didn't expect and they already paid for. Thrill your customers and watch your referrals increase and word-of-mouth spread!"

To learn more about Joel Weldon's sales expertise, view his Web site at http://www.successcomesincans.com.

10

EXCEED YOUR SALES GOALS

"Hold yourself responsible for a higher standard
than anyone else expects of you."
HENRY WARD BEECHER

Y ou are capable of exceeding any goal you set your mind to. Yet to exceed your goals, you'll probably first need to think and act differently than you do right now. Once you set your intentions, and then work toward those intentions, you will be planting the seeds required to grow your success.

The seeds are the ideas and reasons behind your goals. How can you achieve your goals, much less exceed them, if they are not yet defined as to why they are important to you? You can't.

Exceeding goals takes laser-beam focus, courage, knowledge, expertise, 110 percent of your efforts, self-confidence, and, of course, a positive belief system. You will achieve what you believe you absolutely deserve. What this means is that you must be totally committed to skyrocketing past your previous sales records.

GET STARTED BY WRITING YOUR GOAL LIST

Setting goals alone is more than most people do in life. If you write down your goals and review them frequently, you are well on your way to accomplishing what you want. Writing out your goals will help you to develop good working habits and allow you to become more self-disciplined at the same time.

When obstacles get in your way, you will need real drive, determination, and commitment to keep going and to not give up. Determine the reasons for really wanting to accomplish your goals. Add timely and specific plans to your list. This will give you more drive and power to turn them into reality.

Proper goal setting and good execution of your goals will automatically move away obstacles that get in your way. Once your goals have been set, you can begin to translate them into positive action. Prioritize your goals to help you organize your work and stay on track. Begin to do things in order of importance. Prioritize your actions every day.

Goal-minded salespeople never take their minds off of long-range goals, because the penalty (short-term frustrations) can wipe out a haphazard plan. It's simple and highly effective to write down your goals. Yet, more than 80 percent of all salespeople work without a plan to follow. Many of these salespeople without goals are running in a lot of different directions and not staying focused on the goals that could be keeping them growing and improving.

Mark V. Hanson, coauthor of the best-selling book *Chicken Soup for the Soul*, taught me how to develop the POWER of writing down my goals. He told me to write down 101 goals. Wow, 101 goals—that would take me forever! But Mark told me that it would be easy if I relaxed, put on some calming music, rid myself of any outside distractions, and just started writing. Don't think about it too much or get too detailed when you start writing out your list. Just get words on paper. Once your list is completed, you can go back and prioritize, date, and add in the details. Your list can include both short-term and long-term goals.

Taking his advice, I put on an Enya CD, relaxed, and began to get inspired. As I typed away on my computer, I didn't stop to take my fingers off the keyboard or look up. I stayed focused on what I wanted in my personal life and in my professional life. As I got into my goal zone, ideas began to flow easily, just like Mark had promised. Some ideas and goals came out of me that I was not even aware I actually wanted until I saw them in black and white.

Within 20 minutes, I already had a list of 110 things I wanted to accomplish and achieve. Whoa! I never knew I wanted so much. I even removed 9 of the goals from my list because I had too many.

When you sit down to write out your List of 101 Goals, be open and free with ideas. Allow your mind to be set free. Move away from your conscious thoughts and allow your subconscious brain to kick in and offer up suggestive ideas that your conscious mind does not have to judge and analyze. Simply let your thoughts flow onto the page. If you prefer to compose your list on your computer, this works too, and will make it easy for you to cut and paste your goals when you prioritize your list.

Don't take a break—just keep going until you have all 101 goals on your list. Don't spend too much time thinking about why and how you want to achieve your goals at first, just keep going until you've finished your list.

Once you have your list of goals, you can then, and only then, begin to discover why you want to achieve them. Next, prioritize your goals and list them in order of importance. Finally, add the date by which you plan to complete each goal on your list. Be realistic, but stretch yourself at the same time.

Being the overachiever that I am, all of the items on my list were goals to be achieved within one year's time. Your list can include goals for one year up to five years. But make sure to prioritize them in order from short-term to long-term goals.

Within just one hour of starting, I had completed, prioritized, and dated 101 goals. I discovered that the experience was empowering, fun, and exciting. It was an amazing self-indulgent exercise that made me feel like I was watching an inspirational movie of what my life was to become. I was visualizing my future dreams, inspirations, and desires.

You'll enjoy these same feelings when you allow yourself to get in the goal zone too. Be completely open to allowing ideas, dreams, and aspirations to flow easily from your mind. Stay relaxed and nonjudgmental. Allow yourself to get in a focused state and let your subconscious mind feel free to do its work.

I've heard that if you write down your goals, even if you never look at them again, you can achieve up to 80 percent of everything on the list. How is this possible? It's possible, because when you write out your goals, you fill your subconscious mind with thoughts, and it immediately goes to work to take action to turn those thoughts into reality. Setting your goals lets you train your belief system to allow you to take actions to make your goals a reality.

I did not think that this was possible until it happened to me. After I wrote my List of 101 Goals, I got so busy that I had forgotten about it. It was not until six months later that I remembered my list and took time to review it to see what I might have accomplished. It was amazing! I had achieved 70 percent of the goals on my list, and only six months had past. Some of them I had completely forgotten about, and others were no longer important to me. And the most exciting thing of all was that I had exceeded the expectations of several of the goals on my list. It was an exciting and empowering reward!

The power of goal writing truly is amazing! Once you feed your brain, it starts working for you in amazing ways. You are what you think—so think BIG and allow your mind to help you exceed your goals.

For example, one of the personal goals that I added to my list was to visit Paris. Going to Paris was a dream of mine for most of my adult life. After spending 15 years in the fashion retail industry, I was eager to visit the shops and cafés of Paris. I was even decorating my new home Parisian style.

Although I had added this dream to my goal list, it was at the bottom of my priorities because I didn't believe that it was a very realistic goal for me to achieve at this time in my life. After all, I had just walked away from a six-year, personal relationship just a month before. Now here I was writing down a goal to visit the most romantic city in the world, at a time when I was single for the first time in years. On top of that, I had just purchased a new home and new furniture, and I couldn't afford to go. I believed it made no sense, but I wrote the goal down anyway. I really wanted to go there someday, and I knew that if I added it to my list it would make it appear more realistic.

Within a few weeks of writing out my goal list, I had shared some of my goals with my mom. Knowing that affirmations allow you to visualize, solidify, and achieve goals faster, I trusted in sharing my goals and asking for her support. I told her of my dream to visit Paris within the year knowing it was a crazy thing to hope for.

"Did you know that your brother and sister-in-law are going to France in two months?" she responded. What? "They are going to spend a week in the South of France and then a week in Paris." What? I couldn't believe what she had just said, because my brother had never traveled overseas in his life. And he was going to be in Paris?

I asked if she was sure. "Yes, they already have their tickets, and they plan on renting an apartment in downtown Paris to spend the second week touring the sites of the city."

First I thought, well, I'm going to meet them in Paris. I just have to. This is my opportunity! Then my conscious, rational mind kicked in and I thought, No wait, I can't go. I can't afford to go right now. And why would I want to visit such a romantic city without a man to share it with?

Then my savvy woman of the world, realistic mind-set kicked in. Well, of course, I could go. In fact, I had so many frequent flyer miles that I could fly first class for free. I adore spending time with my family, so why would I think that I need a man to go to Paris? Bonjour! The next day I booked my ticket, and within two months, was having one of the best vacations of my life in fabulous, charming, romantic Paris. Ooh, la, la!

Never underestimate the POWER of writing out your goals!

Stop! Put this book down and take the time right now to sit down and write out your List of 101 Goals. I'll be right here waiting for you when you return.

Once you've completed your list, here are some steps that will allow you to achieve those goals even faster.

SIX STEPS TO HELP YOU EASILY ACHIEVE YOUR GOALS

Step #1: Be persistent. Persistence and goal setting play a big role in achieving sales success. But before you focus on your goals, determine what your purpose is first. Salespeople need to be clear about the purpose of achieving goals.

Your purpose is what you feel compelled to do or to accomplish, and it's what keeps you on course. It's what gives meaning and direction to your career. So the first step is not to come up with a string of goals, it is to clarify your purpose and then get more specific. Your goals need to be consistent with that purpose. Otherwise, you're not going to have the passion and enthusiasm you need to go out and exceed the goals you set for yourself.

Step #2: Ensure victory with simple and short-term goals first. Always have some goals that are easy to reach. Simple goals and short-term goals will motivate you as you achieve them, and they will keep you headed toward your larger goals.

Step #3: Share your goals as affirmations. Speaking your goals out loud in the form of affirmations will not only help to feed your own subconscious mind, it also will allow others to support your efforts too. You are more likely to achieve your goals if your friends, business associates, and family know about them. Only share your goals with people who will encourage your growth and success, and be sure to avoid negative forces.

It always amazes me how many goals I achieve by sharing them with others. My friends, family, business associates, and even my audience attendees help me stay on track and keep me moving toward my goals with continuous positive encouragement.

If you have a tendency to disappoint yourself before disappointing others, you may not feel comfortable sharing your goals. Yet, most people who don't share their goals often don't really believe that they can accomplish them. Any negative self-doubt will feed your beliefs and sabotage the results of your goals. To avoid this, start by sharing short-term goals first, then move on to more long-term or riskier goals as you feel more confident with your sales success.

Step #4: Prioritize—yet be flexible. It is best to decide which goals are most important for you to achieve. Date your goals accordingly in the areas that will reap you the largest return on your investment of time and effort. Ask yourself if a task is moving you toward your goals faster or holding you back from skyrocketing your sales potential.

Be open and flexible to changes around you. Due to unforeseen circumstances, you may need to adjust the due date of your goal or reevaluate and cancel it altogether. Often, the goals that receive the most attention are most likely the ones that will change frequently too.

Understand why you want to achieve and exceed your goals. Why will exceeding your goals make your life better than it is right now? Clarify the root of why you want to exceed your goals. Is it to earn respect from others or to create a better lifestyle for your family? Will your goal have a profound impact on your life or on others? Will exceeding your goals help you win the sales awards you've always dreamed of winning?

Step #5: Don't let your ego get in the way of setting big goals.   Don't ever allow your ego to stand in the way of seeking new ideas and advice that can help you exceed your goals. The ego can often drive us to keep doing the same unproductive things, and unreasonably keeps us hoping for different, productive results. The ego very often gets in the way of one professional asking for the advice of peers or colleagues. Don't let your ego get in the way of asking for help and support. You can't do it on your own. You need the support, secrets, and strategies of someone who's been there and done that before you.

Step #6: Don't give up.   You will get discouraged from time to time, and may even start to doubt yourself. That is just human nature. You also will get busy and sidetracked, and may have a tendency to procrastinate. But don't stop! Keep moving toward your goals—one step at a time.

NO MORE EXCUSES—GO FOR IT!

Salespeople often are paid based fully or partially on their performance. You'll never get rich working in an hourly job or on straight salary. But if you create a situation that allows you to get paid based on your sales results, your opportunities will soar. Selling is one of the highest-paid professions. If you are good at it, you can write your own paycheck and make a fortune at it.

There is nothing wrong with wanting more. Set yourself up to believe that you are truly worthy of a higher level of success.

To get more and exceed more, you must S-T-R-E-T-C-H yourself. To exceed and maximize your growth and potential quickly, you must develop some goals that scare you. Yes, scare you! If you are not scaring yourself with some of your sales and success goals, then you are not stretching yourself far enough outside of your comfort zone.

Move past your fears. The reason many salespeople do not set goals is the fear of failure. Yet the only true failure is to not attempt to try new things or to set new goals. If you don't try, you'll never reap the rewards. If you try and only partly succeed, you still will be a success, and you will have achieved more than you've got right now.

There are frequently a variety of obstacles that keep people from achieving and exceeding their potential. The largest obstacle of all is the fear of failure. Underachieving salespeople think to themselves, "If I try to go to the next level, I could fall on my face, embarrass myself, or be exposed as not having the potential that everyone thinks I have."

Other obstacles that hold salespeople back from reaching their goals are procrastination, the fear of success, discouragement, and the lack of commitment to make decisions. It is almost impossible to take decisive action that will allow you to exceed goals if you allow unresolved issues and conflicts to get in the way.

If your goals aren't a little far-fetched and scary at times, they are probably not stretching you to your full potential. Pay attention to this, because this is when boredom can set in. Once boredom sets in, you lose your motivation, drive, and determination. If you are not doing things that support your vision and your goals, you're staying stuck or falling behind.

We all have different levels of comfort. We do, think, and act habitually on those things that we have already easily accomplished. We don't doubt those accomplishments, skills, or habits because they make us feel safe. We all have limited levels of comfort that hold us back from exceeding our goals. Even the most successful people have some level of comfort. But the difference between successful people and people who are not successful is that they push forward despite their fears. They accept change quicker and PUSH themselves outside of their comfort zones time and time again with each level of success they achieve.

If your comfort zone level is not making you feel as if you are growing, learning, and exceeding your goals to achieve the desired outcomes you wish for, they still hold you back. This is what I call an uncomfortable comfort zone. The fear of doing things that stretch your comfort zone level is probably causing you the pain of not getting what you truly want.

To achieve and exceed the goals that you truly want, you must take risks that move you outside of the comfort zone you are currently in. Move outside of it, around it, over it, and through it! Quit being afraid, quit making excuses, and just go for it! Once you overcome a fear, you instantly will feel more empowered.

VISUALIZE YOUR SALES GOALS

Here's a formula for success: Write down your goals, share them with others, and visualize your success before it happens.

Whatever you see, hear, and experience from your past and current sales situations equals your beliefs and the information you currently possess.

If you are not clear on how you will achieve your goals both visually and mentally, how can you achieve them? You only see things that are in alignment with what you already believe. If you don't believe you can exceed your goals, you won't see enough opportunities to get you there. And even when you do see opportunity, you will undermine your own efforts with negative self-talk that holds you back and keeps you stuck.

Begin your vision with the end in mind. What is the result that you want? Give yourself the freedom to visualize BIG. Picture a compelling goal that you really want. How you make it happen is not important right now. Start by thinking about what it is that you most want. You can break down the how-to steps of getting there later. Start by first focusing on what you want.

Sales goals must be expressed in ways that compel you to achieve them. The human brain directs us toward creating what we focus on, good or bad. Start by writing down your goal. The more specific you make your goal the better. Create the picture in your mind and write down specific quantities, dates or time periods, places, people, etc.

Now make the image of your goal really compelling. Visualize it with color, sound, and senses. Once you figure out what you want, get clear and create BIG reasons why you want not only to achieve it, but also to exceed it.

Here's an example. Let's say your vision is to make three times the amount of money you are making right now. That would be a BIG goal, but it's still not specific enough. Define why you want to make this income and when you plan on achieving it. When you visualize those things as well, you'll have a goal that is specific, focused, and timed.

A good time to practice visualization or mental imagery is just prior to going to sleep. Sit down in a quiet spot, relax, close your eyes, and begin to create mental pictures and strong visualizations that move you to future success. What is it like at that place? How do you feel? What do you see yourself achieving? How do others positively respond to your results?

The good thing about visualization is that it goes directly to your subconscious mind—the place where your beliefs have been reinforced for years. These beliefs have been reinforced in your mind for the past 20, 30, or 40+ years. It takes work to change, but daily visualization will take you on the path to making it happen quicker.

Make sure that your vision is clear and your affirmation is focused on where you want to go. The more you affirm that it is important that you change to achieve the goals you truly want, the more you feed your subconscious to make it happen for you.

Don't try—do!

Be willing to expand your thoughts on what you can achieve and accomplish. Think expansively and learn to expand your mind to think bigger and bolder. Be reasonable, but allow miracles to happen to you at the same time by not setting limits on yourself.

The more you understand why you want something, the more motivated you will be to keep working at accomplishing and exceeding your goals. So what is the reason you have to exceed your goal? Maybe the answer is that by exceeding your goal it will make you feel more successful, powerful, and capable. Or you may say that you will be able to afford a nice home or car, or have financial independence at an early age.

Stop right now and ask yourself some reflective questions. As you begin to reflect on where you are now, you will allow yourself to set realistic goals that you can visualize and easily obtain.

- Do I feel that I am limiting my sales potential now?
- If so, how am I currently limiting your success?
- What could I do that will stretch me outside of my comfort zone?
- What scares me, but also excites me about selling?
- If I were to move past my biggest obstacle, what would it be?

- What motivates me to achieve and then exceed my goals?
- Why do I want to exceed my goals?
- How will I exceed my goals this month and every month?

Make a copy of these questions and begin to journal your reflections and beliefs each month. Keep reflecting on, and coming back to, these questions until you have developed new habits and have programmed your subconscious mind to work for you.

With a clear, confident, and predictive vision, you'll see dramatic improvement in exceeding your goals. The power of your own visualization and laser-beam focus is within you.

Don't just sit back and wait for sales to come your way. Focus your positive beliefs and actions toward creating opportunities that will allow you to exceed your goals now!

GO FOR QUALITY PROSPECTS

If you don't have customers who are helping you to exceed your goals—get some new customers!

I learned that to exceed my goals as a professional speaker, I had to move away from a lot of customers over the years. Every time I felt that my expertise, knowledge, skill, and opportunities had grown, I would raise my speaking fees. When I raised my fees, I had to lose some of my customers who could no longer afford to hire me.

Now I could have kept my fees the same, kept all the same customers, and picked up some new customers too, if I wanted to work hard at exceeding my goals. But working harder at this point in my career was not what I had in mind. Instead, I chose to work smarter at exceeding my goals. And you should too.

Moving away from customers you already have to seek out more qualified prospects you don't yet have, is not an easy thing to do—it takes some guts. You must have the confidence in your abilities to trust that moving away from them and focusing on more qualified buyers is the right thing for you to do.

You may or may not have the opportunity to move away from some of your existing customers right now. Maybe you just started your sales career and need all the warm bodies you can find. If that is the case, then by all means keep working hard to meet, greet, and connect with every prospect you can. But if you have been in sales for a while or own your own business, upscaling your customer base may be one of the best ways to go about exceeding your existing goals.

Okay, let's look at this concept another way. Let's say you're not new to sales, but you are not in a sales position that allows you to move away from any of your existing customers. If this is the case, you have two choices: you can either stay in your same position and work harder year after year, or you can move away from your position and find another sales career that will allow you to make more commission and/or allow you to focus on a more upscale customer, product, or service. It's your choice to either work harder or work smarter. Both will help you to exceed your goals as long as you stay focused on them. But by working smarter, you allow yourself more time to work with a more qualified customer who can buy more from you, instead of chasing down prospects who can't afford to invest in what you have to offer. Finding the RIGHT customers and prospects is KEY to your sales success.

With the use of the extra time and effort spent on gaining and working with more qualified customers, you will quickly skyrocket your sales and exceed your goals.

The smartest sales professionals call only those prospects who have expressed great interest and are likely to buy. They create systems that get more prospective warm leads coming their way. It's a leg up in developing a positive selling environment. Most of these warm leads easily generate positive expectations and pleasant experiences.

When you develop a built-in system that continually brings in more warm leads, you automatically attract and obtain highly qualified prospects. By doing this, you not only wipe away time lost on poorly qualified prospects, you develop more quality leads and enjoy selling more. Setting up marketing systems that bring you more quality leads will automatically improve your success at making more sales.

Stay focused, keep learning, take action, and keep moving forward one step at a time.

11

NOW THE
REAL WORK BEGINS

*"Relationships of trust depend on our willingness to look not only
to our interests, but also the interests of others."*
PETER FARQUHARSON

Let your customers know that you truly care by showing them after the sale is completed. Staying in touch with your existing customers and new prospects is an ongoing process and should never be taken lightly. If you don't focus on getting more business from your existing customers and instead focus more on getting new leads, you will lose out on a ton of repeat business.

You've probably heard the saying: "It's easier to keep an existing customer than to get a new one." If this is true, then why do so many salespeople throw away business with customers who already love them? Because it is in a salesperson's nature to always "chase" new leads!

Yet the number one reason why customers don't return to buy from someone with whom they have already done business is not because they didn't like them—it is because they forgot about them. Are your customers forgetting about you, or are you staying in touch with them on a continuous basis?

IT'S HARD TO GET GOOD SERVICE

When I ask people in my audience what makes their business stand out from their competitors, they often say, "We offer great customer service!" When this happens, I ask the rest of my audience to raise their hands if they offer great customer service too. Almost every hand flies high up in the air enthusiastically. This always amazes me, because if everyone believes they provide the best customer service, why is there so much BAD customer service out there? You know it to be true, because you get bad service much of the time too.

So if we are all getting bad service—your customer is getting bad service too. That's the problem. With bad service, poor quality, and a lack of accountability by some salespeople, customers now have the perception that it is hard to get good service. They also believe that there's not much they can do about it either. In fact, they sometimes expect to get burned by poor service before it ever actually happens. Unfortunately, until you prove otherwise, customers are just waiting for you to mess up too.

Due to bad experiences in the past, your customers have been programmed not to believe what salespeople tell them. But now you have the opportunity to WOW them with follow-up and follow-through. You have the opportunity to change their beliefs and build trust in you and your organization.

Customers don't want to be badgered, but they want to know they won't be forgotten after the sale has gone through. Provide good follow-up, yet respect your customer's privacy at the same time. Tell the customer you are going to stay in touch, and ask them how they would like you to stay in touch (by phone, e-mail, mailers, etc.). Don't assume that you know how the customer would like you to follow up—ASK them instead.

As important as it is to build trust during the sales process, it is equally important, if not more important, to build trust again after the sale.

You have a huge responsibility and task in changing your customers' perception of poor service, and you and your organization must set the highest standards possible. To do this, you must offer them extraordinary service—not just ordinary service. With today's savvy and skeptical customers, you must WOW THEM to win their trust after the sale.

The best way to do this is to ASK them how you can improve. Even when they tell you they are 100 percent satisfied with the service you provided, you still need to ASK. Ask them for feedback using a simple and straightforward approach. Listen intently and discover what really works for them. Learn why they want to do business with you in the future and/or refer you to other people that they know. When you discover this, you'll uncover a gold mine of repeat business and referrals. Don't ever assume that your customers will return on their own, no matter how much they love you. Jut because they love you today, doesn't mean that another competitor won't steal them away tomorrow.

To find out more about your customers, you can ASK them to complete an in-store survey, an online survey, or a direct mail survey. But don't ask your customers to give you detailed feedback without offering them something in return. It really bugs me when I get a lengthy survey form in the mail asking me to help the company improve their service, with no respect for my valuable time. I have even received surveys in the mail without even so much as a self-addressed envelope. Now that is just wrong! When you ask your customers to give you feedback in any way—always reward!

Tell your customers that you greatly appreciate that they care about you and your organization enough to take a few minutes from their very valuable time to complete the enclosed survey. Create the assumption that they will be completing the form. Then give them a good reason for taking their valuable time to give you feedback. Your customers' feedback will be priceless in helping you quickly improve your customer service skills.

In your letter, discuss how you plan on rewarding them when they return the survey form to you. And by all means, add a self-addressed, stamped envelope, or an e-mail link if you are sending the information online. Your customer's feedback will give you all the tools you will need to market to them again, as well as to market effectively to new prospects.

Here are some ideas on how to reward your customers for their feedback:

- Set up a contest to win a big grand prize each month.
- Offer in-store discount coupons.
- Give away free tickets for lunch or dinner at a local restaurant.
- Offer free movie tickets.
- Mail back a video store gift certificate and popcorn.
- Give a gift certificate to a local coffee shop.

Here are ten questions you may want to ASK when getting feedback:

1. Why did you do business with our company instead of with our competitors?
2. From the experience you had with our sales department, would you return to do business with us again?
3. What areas can our sales department improve on?
4. What is one of the best experiences you've ever had with a salesperson?
5. What made the experience stand out as extraordinary?
6. What is one of the worst experiences you've ever had with a salesperson?
7. Do you have any feedback on how our team answered the phone when you called?

8. How can we improve the quality of our service and/or products?
9. Would you refer our service or products to your friends and family?
10. What else could we do to improve on our customer service?

Customers will be happy that you ASKED for their advice and opinions, and most likely will be happy to offer it to you. At the same time, they will probably add a lot of things you are doing right on the survey or in the conversation as well. You always can learn how to improve and get better. Be open to improving on a continuous basis.

You easily will improve your service by quickly implementing customer ideas and new service strategies. This invaluable feedback will help you to be EXTRAORDINARY!

Maxwell Funding Group out of Phoenix, Arizona, is the mortgage company that my partners and I use for all of our real estate investments. Avery Maxwell (owner of Maxwell Funding) developed an innovative, follow-up strategy that has produced extremely positive results and has really WOWED my investors and me. Avery believes that to be successful it is imperative to make a lasting impression. Avery's way of going the extra mile, for ALL of his clients, is by throwing what I like to call "Avery's Housewarming Parties."

The power of ASKING is amazing. That is why I keep referring to it throughout this book. To make this amazing power work for you, you must get in the habit of asking for 50 percent more than you have right now. Hey, even if you are a LOUSY ASKER, you'll probably get 25 percent more than you've already got. Get in the habit of asking for more every day. Ask and you shall receive! ASK for the sale, ASK for referrals, ASK for repeat business, and ASK for testimonials for your marketing materials—ASK! ASK! ASK!

Once his clients have moved into their new home and had a chance to settle in, Avery follows up with them to see if they would like Maxwell Funding to throw a housewarming party. Avery's company does everything from sending out the invitations to delivering the food. The entire process is simple. All the client needs to provide is a guest list and preference of food and beverage, that's it!

I believe this idea is absolutely ingenious! Everyone wants their friends and family to come over to see their new home, but who has the time once they've moved in? Most people either wait too long or forget about having a party altogether. Maxwell Funding understands that buying a home is an emotional experience, and they pride themselves on making the entire process run smoothly and with the least amount of stress as possible.

Avery puts on his housewarming parties for absolutely free. Now you may be thinking that would be an expensive gift to give every client, but think again. Avery's company is not *spending* money on their clients, rather, they are *investing* innovative marketing dollars on customers who already know and trust them. In addition, his organization reaps the rewards of endless referrals. Where can you guarantee that kind of return from an advertisement or direct mail piece? You can't! This strategy has low costs with maximum results.

Avery and Martin Vacco, director of marketing, attend every one of these events. Now you also may be thinking, "How does he find the time to set up these events much less attend them?" Well let's just say that Avery's organization has a priority for investing in their clients who already love working with them—as opposed to chasing down new prospects, which can be very time consuming. These parties create the perfect opportunity for his organization to get instant referrals from his client's friends and family in a comfortable, relaxed atmosphere.

HOLDING ON TO CUSTOMER RESPECT

Will your customers respect you in the morning?

Follow-up and follow-through are two business strategies that most salespeople tend to ignore. They spend a lot of time, money, and effort chasing down new customers, only to lose them after the first or second transaction. The main reason this happens is because they don't follow up and they don't follow through after the sale. Therefore, the customer doesn't feel appreciated or easily can do business with another competitor. The salesperson has given them no reason to make their company the one and only choice for continued business.

Your customers already have been burned so many times by bad service that they are shocked when salespeople actually follow up and follow through with their business mission. Think of how you feel when you do business with a company that does not follow through on their promises.

It is easy to overcome this by raising the bar of follow-up and follow-through before, during, and after the sale. Don't settle for less than your best, even follow up on your follow-up. Always give your customers more than they expect, every time they do business with you. Create a personal mission statement and include the motto of thinking and feeling follow up and follow through with every customer, every day, every time they do business with you.

It is easy to think of follow-up as sending thank-you notes and connecting by phone or e-mail. These contacts are important, but they are not the bottom line. When following up, there are three areas you can't afford to ignore:

1. The desire to move ahead. Do you have the will to take care of your customers in your heart, body, and mind? Do you truly care about your customers, and are you willing to do whatever it takes to keep those customers for life? It is the ability to stay focused and concentrate on the task

at hand that will determine your results. Do you have a belief so strong that failure is not an option to you?

2. Taking the relationship to the next level. Discover new ways to reach out to your customers. Take steps to improve from the customer's perspective. Consider their benefits and needs. Ask your customers how they would like you to follow up, and what you can do to improve your service. Ask them why they enjoy doing business with YOU. Again, ask them how they would like you to communicate with them. Think about who your customer is, what they need most, and how you can best meet those needs, and your follow-up and follow-though will come naturally, because you will be following the customer's agenda, not yours.

3. Take steps to enhance your customer growth. How can you build your relationship beyond the first sale? Think of each new customer as a lifetime customer, no matter what the size of the sale. Most people think of follow-up as a system to ensure that everything gets done. That is only a small part of it. Follow-up is what you do to ensure that you build the strongest, longest lasting relationships possible. Your enthusiasm will determine your success. Combine this with the benefits you offer your customers, and you will take the most effective steps to follow up and follow through.

Follow **U**p to **B**uild **G**ood **S**ales **R**elationships

Jay Conrad Levinson, author of the *Guerrilla Marketing* series, offers the following advice:

"First, be sure to follow up as soon as possible. That used to mean within a week, then within two days. Now it means within 24 hours, or better still, within 2 hours.

The reason for your first follow-up should be to thank your customer.

Follow up again within a week to see if the customer has any questions.

Follow up again three months later and offer something for sale that's related to the customer's last purchase.

Then follow up after another three months, again offering something that you know your customer will be interested in. At the three month mark, follow up to give them information about the worth and value of your products or services.

At the end of one year, send an anniversary card celebrating the one-year anniversary of your customer being your customer. Do this every year and you'll see your relationship blossom.

It's the instant follow-up and consistent follow-up that will give you the warm relationship for which you must strive."

Jay Conrad Levinson is the father of *Guerrilla Marketing* and the author of the *Guerrilla Marketing* series of books, which have sold more than 14 million copies and have been published in 41 languages. Check him out at http://www.gmarketing.com or log on to his Web site at http://www.guerrillamarketingassociation.com.

APPRECIATION GOES A LONG WAY

Always show and tell your customers how much you truly appreciate their business. Don't assume that they don't want to hear it from you—because they do! One of the most magical words your customer can hear is their own names. Get in the habit of repeating your customer's name a few times during a sales presentation. This will make your connection more personal and much more powerful.

Debbie Bermont, author of *Outrageous Business Growth: The Fast Track to Explosive Sales in Any Economy*, says that people will come back to buy from you if they feel valued, appreciated, and special. When they remember an exceptional experience they will give you their money again and again in return for that special treatment. You will never have to worry about your competition if you make your customers feel that they are special through your words, actions, customer policy, and follow-up.

Always follow up with a greeting card or handwritten note thanking them for their business. This gesture will help you to stand out from your competitors because few of them are taking the time to do it, and the few who do are not doing so consistently.

What is the first thing you open when you have a pile of mail in front of you? Probably something that is personalized or handwritten. Right? You look at this first because it doesn't come across as salesy. Instead, it comes to you in the form of personalization. It is something directly and specifically to YOU.

SALES OPPORTUNITIES LOST WHEN THE PHONE RINGS

When the phone rings in your business, are you and your team prepared to turn the call into a solid sales opportunity? Or are you and your team rushing through the call, not connecting with prospective customers, and losing you thousands of dollars in sales revenue in return?

How many businesses do you call that WOW you on the phone? How many actually take the time to connect with you and use the opportunity to market their business more effectively? This always amazes me, because most businesses spend countless dollars on advertising, hoping customers will call them, but when they do, customers are often put on hold or put off.

Hold Please!

You know how frustrating it is when you call a business and before you can get a word out, you hear, "Can you hold please?" Most of the time, you don't even have time to respond and they already have you on hold. So why did they even bother asking?

You didn't call to be put on hold or transferred three times, explaining your question or concern over and over. Then, when you finally think you've been heard, you hear, "Sorry you've got the wrong department. I'll need to transfer you. Can you hold please?" ERRRRRR!

Voice Mail Hell

The only thing worse than being put on hold is going through voice mail hell. Will a REAL LIVE person ever answer the phone? Often, there are so many choices on the voice mail that you forget what you called for, and then the message comes on and says, "To repeat this messages press . . . ." Then you go through it all over again until, finally, you reach the right person in the right department and they say, "Can you hold please?" ERRRRR!

Do these people ever call their own companies to see how their prospective customers are being turned off every day? I doubt it!

When you have to place your customers on hold, use this as a marketing opportunity. Instead of keeping them on hold with boring silence, use this as an opportunity to market what you sell. Record live testimonials from your best customers and let them sell YOU. Mix the testimonials in with up-to-date promotional offers, Web site information, and the like. The recorded message will entertain your customers while they wait, give them more information about what you have to sell, and presell the benefits of doing business with you instead of your competition.

"Call Your Own Business" Challenge

When discussing lost sales opportunities in my presentations, I ask for volunteers that would allow me to call their businesses in front of the audience. Some brave business owner always steps up to the challenge. They call their business from their cell phone and hand it over to me. I get on the call posing as a prospective customer. At the same time, the entire audience on the microphone hears the call. Most of the time, they are shocked by what employees have to say.

During one presentation, the owner of a company who sold sandals wholesale had a warehouse in the city where I was presenting. He made the call and handed me the phone. I explained to the employee that I understood they were wholesalers, but wondered if he could tell me of a retail store in the area that sold their shoes. After the employee told me he was not sure, he put me on hold. When he returned, he told me, "No, sorry. We don't have anyone in town." I said, "Okay. Well I live in Scottsdale, Arizona. Do you know of a store that sells them there? I really want to buy a few pairs because I think they're great." He then replied, "No, I don't think we have a store there either. I really don't know which retailers carry our shoes."

Yikes! The business owner sat there in shock as he heard the conversation. When I hung up, he told me how upset that call made him because they had a couple of retail stores in the area, plus some in my city as well. He thanked me for making him aware of how much they needed to improve.

Whose fault was it that the sales opportunity was lost: the employee or the owner? Both, because if the owner never communicated to his employees how to handle calls or never went through different scenarios to allow the employees to think on their feet, how would they ever know how to do it, much less how to do it well?

Studies Reveal More Lost Opportunities

Studies consistently show that the telephone remains one of the most underused business tools. Researchers called 5,000 Yellow Pages advertisers to say that they had seen their ad, and asked about the price of their products or services.

The results revealed endless lost opportunities, including the following:

- More than 78 percent of those phoned didn't bother asking for the caller's name. Lost opportunity!
- More than 55 percent took eight rings or more to answer.
- According to the researchers, many of the people who answered the phone rushed through the call and spoke so rapidly that it was hard to understand them. Lost opportunity!
- Less than 10 percent answered the phone in a manner that made the caller feel welcome enough to want to do business with them. Lost opportunity!

Your telephone can be a powerful selling tool if you and your team regard every call as a sales opportunity. When leaving a recording, make it sound as conversational and friendly as possible. Record your message standing up. Speak with energy and enthusiasm, and put a smile in your voice.

Create a First Impression Opportunity

Answer the phone by the second or third ring. Taking too long to answer creates an impression of disorganization and/or lack of interest.

Speak slowly and clearly, giving your name, your company's name, and a simple, direct offer of welcome and assistance, such as, "How may I be of assistance to you today?"

Put a smile on your face when you pick up the phone, and a smile in your voice before you reply. To get into the habit of doing this, place a mirror next to the phone so that you will see your facial expression when you answer.

What impression are you leaving when you can't get to the call? Are you missing a few messages on your voice mail? It could be the way you greet your callers. Your greeting to the caller needs to give useful information. Obviously, you're away from your desk, so why bother telling the caller that. Get to the point, be creative, give the caller pertinent information, and always mention when you will be returning their call.

When You Are Making the Call

When calling prospects, never start out by asking, "How are you today?" This question screams telemarketer! So don't act like one. Let prospects know why you are calling right away. Don't waste their time. If prospects don't know the purpose of your call within 30 seconds, they simply will lose interest, stop listening, and start looking for a way to get you off the phone.

Remind prospects of your relationship and prove that you are carrying through on what you were asked to do or promised to do. Nothing builds rapport better than a promise kept. Rapport leads to trust, and trust leads to loyal customers.

Are you ringing up sales opportunities or placing them on hold?

KEEPING THEM COMING BACK

You must be committed to providing outstanding service to your customers. I strongly urge you to adopt this belief and to live by it each day throughout your sales career, and never deviate from it. Once you commit yourself to this, you will be on your way to enjoying immense success. Give your customers so much service they'll feel guilty even thinking about doing business with somebody else.

It's been estimated that you have a one-in-two chance to get business from an existing customer, and a one-in-four chance to get business from a customer who has not done business with you for a while. Therefore, once you have developed a satisfied customer, provide extraordinary service. Do everything you can, including back bends if you have to, to keep your happy customers coming back.

Customers want you to exceed their expectations. They want you to let them know that you are willing to go beyond the norm, to make that extra effort. Success comes from discovering more ways to do this, yet this is one of the most overlooked areas in the field of selling.

Always tell your customers how much you appreciate their business.

NETWORK FOR NEW LEADS

It is not what you know, but who you get to know that will lead to the most amazing opportunities. The importance of networking is obvious—to meet more prospects. Yet most salespeople don't do much of it at all. Or if they do, they do it haphazardly and casually instead of doing it as part of their business plan.

The most common excuse for not networking is lack of time. If you are avoiding networking to get leads, ask yourself why you aren't finding the time to do more of it. It's easy to use this excuse, but you can't reap the rewards of more prospects unless you work ON your business as well as IN your business. To work on getting more leads, you must get OUT and meet more people. Selling is a people business. The more people you know and get to know, the more prospects, leads, and referrals you will uncover.

The second reason most people back away from networking is due to a feeling of awkwardness when meeting new people. This is the case for a lot of people, no matter how outgoing they may appear to be in their own work environment. Take them out of that environment and many of them freeze up.

If that sounds like you, and you're feeling uncomfortable in networking situations outside of work, I suggest you join a Toastmasters group. Toastmasters International is one of the oldest networking groups that exist today. It has helped thousands of people develop new skills to build the confidence they need for public speaking. When I joined a small Toastmasters group many years ago, I wanted to learn how to feel more comfortable speaking in front of groups so that I could promote my business at chambers of commerce and women's organizations. Public speaking is a big fear for most people. In fact, it ranks over the fear of drowning.

What amazed me about Toastmasters was that only after about two months of attending and testing some speaking before the group, I was 100 percent more comfortable with networking. After that, I could go up and talk to anyone, anywhere. The confidence that Toastmasters teaches in such a short time is amazing. I highly recommend that if you're in sales, you should join Toastmasters. You can find a group in your area by checking online at Toastmasters.org. Don't think about this or wait until you get around to it—just do it. It will guarantee you more confidence and more sales!

Finally, there is one more reason some people avoid networking, and that is because they feel guilt. Yes, guilt. Some people actually feel underdeserving of others' time, respect, and attention outside of their place of work. These feelings or personal beliefs create a fear that limits their networking opportunities. They also believe (not true by the way) that they have little to offer others in the form of conversation, and therefore have no right to ask and receive from others.

Too frequently we settle for working with the people who are the easiest to reach, not the most effective. Or, if and when most of us go to networking events, we look around for the first person we know so that we can stand around and comfortably talk with them. Right? Yes, I know you've done this, because I've done it too. I consider myself very outgoing, but I don't always feel like talking with strangers. Sometimes I actually need to FORCE myself to network.

Remember why you went to the event in the first place? To meet new people and new prospects. So stick with your plan and FORCE yourself if you have to. The rewards from networking will be well worth it in the form of increased customers and increased sales opportunities.

SUPPORT FRIENDLY COMPETITORS

Most salespeople try to keep all the business to themselves. They think of their competitors as the enemy trying to steal away their customers and prospects. Yet I believe that you should join forces with friendly competitors. If you know that your specialty or niche market is not competition to every salesperson, you also understand that there is enough business to go around. Salespeople who fear their competition don't have a strong enough belief in themselves, or confidence in their own abilities.

Once you have boosted your confidence to a high level of success, you also will begin to understand that what goes around comes around. Whatever energy you put out there comes back to you many times over. It's simple the way the universe works.

If you fear that that it will never come back to you if you share a lead or referrals with your competitors, you're also right. That fear will keep you from sharing and putting it out there, so there will be nothing to send you in return.

I've discovered that the power of sharing leads with my friendly competitors has reaped me tons of new business opportunities. I now live by the motto: Never throw business away!

If you specialize and understand the uniqueness in what you have to sell, you also understand that you can't be everything to everyone. Sometimes passing that business on to another salesperson would be better for the customer because they could service their needs better. Yet that is where most salespeople miss out when referring business to their competitors. Do you believe that if you don't send your prospects to your competitors they will find them on their own? Yes, sure they will. So why not be the hero and refer them instead. When you pass along the referral, make sure to put your name out front so that your competitor knows where the business came from.

I'm sure some of you reading this are thinking, "Yeah sure, I've tried this before, and that salesperson never sent me any business in return." Well I've had the same thing happen to me before too, so I understand where you're coming from. But those are the few competitors who are not the friendly ones, or as I like to say, "They don't play well on the playground." So just don't invite them back to play. Find some other friendly competitors who will play well on the sales playground along with you.

Stop looking at your close competitors as your enemies, because they can actually become your best alliances. After all, you have one BIG thing in common with them—the same target market. Not only do you need to refer them when you're not the right fit, but you also should become the walking/talking Rolodex of your alliances. Never throw business away!

Here's an example of how this worked for me:

After I presented a keynote speech for a client in Melbourne, Australia, she asked me if I knew of another speaker living in Australia who spoke on the same topic and that I could refer her to for their next convention. Now turning away business when I was dying inside to go back to Australia was not easy, but I knew that I would not be the right fit for their next event. You see, in my business, when I'm brought in to be the headliner or keynote speaker, they usually don't bring me back for the next event right away because they've already heard my best stuff. No matter how much the audience loves me, they usually want to see another keynote speaker at the next event. So knowing this, I was open to sharing the lead with one of my competitors.

But there was one big problem: I live on the other side of the world and didn't know any speakers from Australia. At this point, I could have easily told my client, "No, sorry, I don't know of anyone to refer you to." Then I could have selfishly and stupidly hoped she would just call me for another opportunity to come back for the next event.

Instead, I went back to the motto I live by: Never throw business away! Today you can find anyone, anywhere on the Internet. Knowing this, I told my client that I would find her someone. I found my client the perfect speaker by doing an online search. I positioned myself in front of my Australian competitor by sending him the lead by e-mail. I didn't know if I would ever hear back from him, but within 24 hours, which is almost instantaneous from Melbourne/Phoenix time, I got an e-mail reply.

This competitor, John Stanley, told me that he was going to be in Phoenix, Arizona, in two weeks, and that he would call me when he arrived. I thought "SURE, a man from the other side of the world was going to be in my hometown." What is the likelihood of that? The likelihood was real—guess it is a small world after all.

When I met with John, he was thankful for the referral, and very open to sharing leads with me. We talked and shared ideas on sending referrals for a couple of hours and, as he would say, "We chatted up a bit." John's generosity still amazes me to this day. From that one e-mail introduction to a man from the other side of the world I had never met, I was rewarded with thousands of dollars in referral business. This newly discovered business alliance has referred me to dozens of clients in five countries around the world.

The same opportunities are waiting for you too if you simply seek them out and ACT on them. Building strong business alliances with friendly competitors is some of the most strategic networking you can do.

Never doubt the power of the universe. What you confidently put out there will be returned to you many times over.

KEEP MOVING FORWARD ONE STEP AT A TIME

There always will be another call to make, another contract to write up, another prospect to meet, and so on. Selling often can become overwhelming, especially when you are focused on exceeding your goals. It takes a lot of work and effort to be your very best and to make it to the top! But trust that if you take just one more step, you will reach your goal. Don't give up—you can't quit—keep moving forward one step at a time.

Don't get overwhelmed with the process of being your best. Sure, that's easy for me to say. Right? Wrong! It's not easy for me to say because I'll admit that I often get overwhelmed, though I do try to step aside and reevaluate the situation when I do. I remember one such time in particular, when I was working harder instead of smarter. I needed to escape. I needed to get away from it all, relieve myself of my own self-imposed stress, and regain my balance.

The only escape I could think of to get completely away from it all was the Grand Canyon, in Arizona. This wonder of the world was about to help me regain my balance and discover a new goal.

> *"Knowledge advances by steps, and not by leaps."*
> **LORD MACAULAY**

I signed up for a wild raft adventure down in the Grand Canyon. Because I only had one week to spend on my vacation, and I wanted to go on a smaller raft for the full adventure of it, I either needed to hike down the canyon or hike out of the canyon. Not being in good physical condition at the time, I decided to get on my treadmill for 15 minutes a day, about a week before I left, to get in shape. Right . . .

Oh, how hard could it be to hike the canyon? I had heard that it took people as long as nine hours to hike out on this trail. But it couldn't be that hard, I thought, I can certainly exceed that goal easily enough. After all, it's just a big hole in the ground, and I can see the bottom. I decided not to worry about it, and planned to hike out when the raft trip and my vacation had ended.

My raft adventure in the canyon was one of the most amazing vacations I've ever been on. What a great place to get back to nature and away from it all. The raft trip was so exciting that I completely forgot about everything that I had left behind at work. It was just the getaway I needed to help me regain my balance—no phones, no customers, no employees, no worries, and no sales goals. A real vacation!

At the end of the trip our raft guide gathered the few of us together who would be hiking out of the canyon. He said: "This will be one of the most physically challenging things that most of you have ever done in your entire life." Yikes, I didn't want to hear that! "But remember that it is mostly mental. If you keep a positive mind-set, you'll make it out without a problem. When it gets hard, take some time to look around at the beautiful Grand Canyon at every level; and remember to enjoy it, you're still on vacation. Keep putting one foot in front of the other, step-by-step until you reach your goal. Your goal is, of course, to get out of the canyon.

"Oh, one more thing: You can't quit! Don't think that you can just quit when it gets difficult. Because if you do, the park rangers will come down and rescue you, bring you back to the top, find out that you are okay, charge you thousands of dollars, and then . . . put you back on the trail where they found you. So you'll want to stay focused on your goal of hiking the entire canyon on your own."

With my 20-pound backpack in tow, I started out of the canyon. I had the positive mind-set-thing down. That was easy for me. I looked around, and everything I saw on my hike out was positive. I saw a mother deer and her two little babies standing so close to me. With the beautiful Grand Canyon in the background, it was a magical moment. A bit later I stopped to take another break and a little squirrel came up and sat right next to me. I fed the cute squirrel trail mix right out of my hand. I was having so much fun that before I knew it the squirrel had eaten my entire bag of trail mix. Oh well, I didn't need it. This was going to be easy. It was just 2½ hours into my hike, and I already had reached the halfway point on the trail at Indian Gardens. Hey, I thought, this isn't bad at all. I can easily finish the hike out of the canyon and exceed my goal in no time.

Right after the halfway point, though, things started to change dramatically. It was getting much hotter in the day. It was summer, and I swear it must have been 198 degrees. The trail was getting steeper and steeper with every step. My positive mind-set instantly changed to a negative mind-set, and I saw completely different things on the second leg of my journey. I saw scorpions, rattlesnakes, and skeletons of previous hikers along the way!

I remembered again what our guide had to say, "You can't quit!" Darn, I really wanted to quit—I wanted it to be over.

What would you do if someone told you that you couldn't give up on your goals? How would you act differently than you are acting right now? What would you do to complete and exceed the goals you currently have?

Remember, you have to keep going . . . you're not there yet!

I kept going, one step at a time toward my goal. Eight hours from when I began my hike out of the canyon, I saw one of the most beautiful sites of all—someone hiking down with an ice cream cone.

It's hard to keep ice cream from melting in hell, so I knew that I had made it to the last switch back and the finish line was just around the corner. I had reached and exceeded my goal.

What will your ice cream cone look like when you have exceeded your goals?

Enjoy the trail with a positive mind-set on your way to the top!

My mission for writing this book was to deliver a strong message to everyone in sales that would support them in trusting in their abilities more than ever before.

My mission is to help YOU build the strongest sales confidence and the most positive belief system possible that will allow you to exceed any goal you set your mind to.

I trust this book has not only opened up your mind to a new way of thinking about selling, but also your heart to a new way of serving your customers. If it has, please pass the word along and refer this book to everyone you know who sells anything!

Thank you. I look forward to personally meeting you along the trail.

Until then, enjoy your journey and keep soaring!

Debbie Allen

Sales

Confessions of Shameless Self Promoters, by Debbie Allen
How to Be a Great Sales Professional, by Nido Qubein
How to Close Every Sale, by Joe Girard
Never Underestimate the Selling Power of a Woman, by Dottie
    Walters
Sales Secrets from Your Customers, by Barry Farber
Sell the Sizzle, by Patricia Drain
Selling with Integrity, by Sharon Drew Morgen
Stop Whining! Start Selling!, by Jeff Blackman
The New Science of Selling and Persuasion, by Bill Brooks
The Psychology of Sales Call Reluctance®, by George Dudley and
    Shannon Goodson
*Throw the Rabbit–The Ultimate Approach to Three-Dimensional
    Selling,* by Joe Bonura
Triggers, by Joe Sugarman

Marketing

Confessions of Shameless Internet Promoters, by Debbie Allen
The Attractor Factor, by Joe Vitale
Guerilla Marketing, by Jay Conrad Levinson

Business

Endless Referrals: Network Your Everyday Contacts into Sales,
   by Bob Burg
Growing Your Business!, by Mark LeBlanc
*Outrageous Business Growth: The Fast Track to Explosive Sales
   in Any Economy,* by Debbie Bermont
The Power of Focus, by Jack Canfield, Mark Victor Hansen,
   and Les Hewitt
The Profit Pump, by Eric Gelb

Communication

How to Be a Great Communicator, by Nido Qubein
Maximum Influence, by Kurt Mortensen

Self-Help

Outsmart Your Brain, by Marcia Reynolds
The New Psycho-Cybernetics, by Maxwell Maltz and updated
   by Dan Kennedy